AWE Awareness Wonder Expectancy

Now Consciously Create Your Personal Universe

John Sullivan

LiiivWell

Ordering Information Quantity sales. Special discounts are available on quantity purchases by corporations, associations, and others.

For details, contact the publisher at the address below.
Publisher: LiivWell
PO Box 2197, Margaret River, Western Australia, 6285
Web: Liiv.One
Email: john@liiv.com.au

ISBN Paperback : 978-1-7644362-1-2
ISBN E-book: 978-1-7644362-0-5
ISBN Audio-book: 978-1-7644363-2-9

To the Universe-- with Awe, Awareness, Wonder, Expectancy
To those, ,hopefully not many more than few, I've wronged, I am
deeply sorry To those precious few that have wronged me, I forgive
you
To the multitudes that have righted me,, and I have righted
To you, the reader
My love to you all

AWE

Awareness Wonder Expectancy

Now Consciously Create
Your Personal Universe

By John Sullivan

Note on Illustrations:

The brain diagrams included in this book are conceptual visualizations designed to illustrate the 'Whole Brain Huddle' and 'OOARR' frameworks. They are metaphorical representations of functional neural characters and are not intended to serve as anatomically precise medical or topographical maps of the brain.

Medical Disclaimer

The information provided in this book is for educational and informational purposes only and is not intended as medical advice. The content is not intended to be a substitute for professional medical advice, diagnosis, or treatment. Always seek the advice of your physician or other qualified health provider with any questions you may have regarding a medical condition. Never disregard professional medical advice or delay in seeking it because of something you have read in this book. The author and publisher specifically disclaim any liability, loss, or risk, personal or otherwise, that is incurred as a consequence, directly or indirectly, of the use and application of any of the contents of this book.

PART 1: AWE AND OBSERVATION

"It was the best of times, It was the worst of times"

Charles Dickens: Quantum Physicist, Cosmologist, Superpositionist

Author: "A Tale of Two Cities"

Tuning Your Consciousness

The Beach, The Navigator, The Boat

Almost every morning, I stand on the sand at Prevelly Beach, here in Margaret River.

About a kilometer to the north, I can see Surfer's Point, where the world's best surfers compete in the Margaret River Pro. Just beyond it, the river mouth opens into the vast, wild Indian Ocean. To the south, I spot the White Elephant cafe, our meeting spot with our wonderful early morning swim companions.

I watch the swells that have traveled thousands of kilometers finally arrive to meet the land.

Standing there, watching the immense, rhythmic power of the waves, I feel the day's "to-do" list simply... dissolve. The nagging concerns, the anxieties, the loops of old conversations—they shrink. They don't vanish, but their weight seems trivial in the face of that vastness.

I feel connected to something ancient, powerful, and profound.

This feeling has a name: AWE.

It is the moment your brain stops grinding and starts humming.

It is a state of pure coherence.

The Many Faces of Awe

Awe is not a single, prescribed experience. It doesn't just happen at the beach.

I have felt it in its most profoundly human form: the moment each of my three children was born. That is the awe of connection, of life itself emerging .

I have felt it in moments of sublime, ridiculous grandeur. Once, my wife Marg and I were at the Sanctuary Lodge at the entrance to Machu Picchu. I found myself in a spa overlooking the ancient citadel, Pisco sour in hand. Marg and our companions, Natalia and Peter, were deep in conversation below. I called down,

"Come up, this is unbelievable!"

They were in their moment and politely declined.

I saw an opportunity. I took my swimmers off and sat naked in a bubbling spa, beholding Machu Picchu. I thought,

'Not even the great Inca would have done this.'

.

And I have felt it in the face of raw, elemental power. Rounding Cape Horn at 4 am in a Force 9 gale, I said to Marg,

"I'm going out on our leeward balcony nude to behold the Cape."

It was... awe-inspiring. (And freezing).

The Fractal

A fractal repeats with infinite detail at any scale. Every morning you choose to move outside into the light, you are wonderfully experiencing a micro-fractal of everything I will endeavour to communicate here in this book (including the acronym I have drawn from Awe - Awareness, Wonder, Expectancy: another "oar" sounding acronym O.O.A.R.R which is short for Observe. Orient. Act. Realise. Reflect:--The Whole Brain Huddle: along with The Sullivan Theory of the Universe).

You are acknowledging that you are a biological creature dependent on the universe, the Quantom, which includes "our" Sun

Allow me an aside for a moment of awe

It is estimated that there are 14 billion trillion sun-like stars in the "observable" universe - the "bubble" of space from which light has had enough time to reach us since the Big Bang. The actual universe, the Quantom, is likely much larger (potentially infinite), meaning the true number of suns could be infinite.

With your steps outside into the morning light, you are acknowledging that you are a conscious creator choosing to engage with the universe (the Act).

You are not waiting for energy to come to you; you are going to The Source, the Universe.

What happens for most of us after such experiences of awe?

We behold that grand ocean or mountain view, we turn our back, and we walk to the car.

Very quickly, the feeling evaporates. The "other" voice kicks in.

"I need to get petrol"

"Have there been any more delays on the house build?"

"Why did I say that stupid thing to my partner the other day?"

This chatter is the sound of your life on auto-pilot. In neuroscience, this is called the Default Mode Network. Let's call this voice The Anxious Navigator.

Listening to this Navigator, we react to everything. We become "Newtonian Reactors"—living a life where every action forces an equal and opposite reaction .

The Boat and The Ocean

Let's return to the ocean—the infinite ocean of the universe we all exist in.

Imagine yourself as a wonderful little boat floating in this universal ocean. Let's give our little boat a name: your Quan.

This is your personal, experienced universe.

If we live in the world of classical Newtonian physics, we find our boat tossed around by the waves. We forget that every boat requires a means of direction. We forget that we are floating in the Quantom—the infinite, energetic ocean of potential .

The simplest implements for steering a little boat are Oars. This book is going to provide you with those oars.

1. Awe (Awareness, Wonder, Expectancies)

2. O.O.A.R.R (Observe, Orient, Act, Realise, Reflect)

Awe is Propulsion: It provides the energy/fuel. Without AWE, you are drifting.

O.O.A.R.R, also pronounced like "oar" is the Rudder: It provides the direction. Energy (AWE) without Direction (OOARR) is you going around and around in circles, getting hit by waves. Direction without Energy is stagnation.

You need both to move the boat - your personal universe, your Quan - in the way you desire.

One of these oars—the emotion of Awe—you already have. You just need to learn to use it.

THE PROCESS

You may laugh, or think:

How can John dare to write about the universe, creation, and consciousness?

The answer is simple: I am not "there." I am in the process.

My early training as a process engineer taught me this: Everything is a process. The creation of the universe is a process. The experience of awe is a process. And consciously creating your personal universe starts with Awe .

For a long time, we treated this feeling as a luxury—a fleeting moment you might get on a vacation if you were lucky.

We were wrong.

Game-changing research led by Dr. Dacher Keltner at UC Berkeley reveals that Awe is a biological necessity. It is the only experience that reliably shuts down the "Default Mode Network"—the part of your brain where that Anxious Navigator lives .

When you feel Awe, your "self" becomes small, and your connection becomes large. The static in your head clears. Your mind opens.

You are now ready to pick up the first oar.

QUANTUM THEORY - WAVES AND PARTICLES

Most of us treat our reality like it is solid and fixed. We think,

"The world is happening to me."

Modern physics tells us something different. You are not a solid object moving through empty space. Stick with me here. Maybe physics was not your favourite subject at school. Physics though is fundamental to our very existence. So it's worth a little bit of intellectual effort on your part to come to grips with this.

If I told you that fundamental physics holds the secrets to success and wellbeing in your life I am sure you would make the effort - the reality is, it does.

Let's consider the waves of quantum physics. The Quantom is an infinite ocean of waves. Every universal wave frequency exists simultaneously right now.

You cannot see these waves, but they are there.

The physicist most famous for the idea that observation collapses the wave is Niels Bohr, along with his younger protégé Werner Heisenberg.

Together in the 1920s, they developed the Copenhagen Interpretation of quantum mechanics. Their work suggested that reality at the subatomic level doesn't exist in a definite state until it is measured.

What They Said

Before their work, physics assumed that the universe was like a clockwork machine—things existed in specific places whether you looked at them or not. Bohr and Heisenberg argued that this is not true for atoms and particles.

- The Wave Function:

They said a particle (like an electron) exists as a "probability wave" (a mathematical description called a wave function). It isn't in Point A or Point B; it is in a "superposition" of being in both places at once.

- The Collapse

When you measure the particle, you force the universe to make a choice. The wave of probabilities "collapses" instantly into a single, definite particle. The Renninger Effect is extremely meaningful, knowledge alone will collapse the wave function.

Key Quotes

- Niels Bohr:

"It is wrong to think that the task of physics is to find out how nature is. Physics concerns what we can say about nature."

(Meaning: We can't know what reality is before we look at it; we can only describe the interaction.)

- Werner Heisenberg:

"What we observe is not nature itself, but nature exposed to our method of questioning."

THE "OBSERVER" AND CONSCIOUSNESS

When physicists say "observation," it is easy to think they mean a human with eyes. Susan Hossenfelder popularised consciousness in this context.

The Famous Critics

Not everyone agreed. Two of the most famous physicists hated the idea of human observation let alone conscious observation:

- Albert Einstein:

He believed reality existed independently of us. He famously argued,

"I like to think that the moon is there even if I am not looking at it."

- Erwin Schrödinger:

He thought the idea of "collapse" was absurd. He created his famous Schrödinger's Cat thought experiment to mock Bohr. He argued that if Bohr was right, a cat in a box could be simultaneously dead and alive until you opened the lid. (Irony: Today, people use the Cat example to teach quantum mechanics, even though Schrödinger invented it to insult the theory!)

MANY WORLDS VERSUS MULTIVERSE THEORIES

The "Many Worlds Theory" suggests the wave never collapses and every possibility actually happens in a parallel universe.

World renowned Professor Stephen Hawking was a strong advocate of the Many Worlds Interpretation (MWI) of quantum mechanics. However, he was critical of the Multiverse Theory derived from string theory and inflation, spending his final years trying to disprove or "tame" it.

The Many Worlds Interpretation (Quantum Mechanics)

Hawkings Verdict: Advocate

This theory, proposed by Hugh Everett III, suggests that every time a quantum event has multiple possible outcomes, all of them happen, each in a separate, branching branch of reality.

- Hawking's Stance:

He was a long-time supporter of this interpretation. He found it to be the most logical way to interpret the mathematics of quantum mechanics without requiring a mysterious "collapse" of the wave function.

In his own words:

When asked about it, he famously said that the theory was

"self-evidently true." To him, the "worlds" were not necessarily parallel physical places you could travel to, but mathematical realities defined by the wave function of the universe.

THE COSMOLOGICAL MULTIVERSE (ETERNAL INFLATION)

Hawkings Verdict: Skeptic / Reformer

This theory suggests that our Big Bang was just one of many, creating an infinite "mosaic" of bubble universes, each potentially having different laws of physics.

Hawking's Stance:

He was not a fan of this version of the multiverse. He believed an infinite multiverse where "anything is possible" was useless because it made the theory untestable and unable to predict anything about our own universe.

His Final Work:

His very last scientific paper (co-authored with Thomas Hertog) was titled

"A Smooth Exit from Eternal Inflation?"

In it, he used complex mathematics (holography) to argue against the infinite multiverse. He tried to prove that the range of possible universes is actually finite and much simpler than previously thought.

Key Quote:

In an interview regarding this final paper, he explicitly stated:

"I have never been a fan of the multiverse. If the scale of different universes in the multiverse is large or infinite the theory can't be

tested."

The "Sliding Doors" Concept (Many Worlds Interpretation)

Excitingly for The Sullivan Theory of the Universe, very recent research surrounding the

Everettian Many Worlds Interpretation

(supported by Hawking, as discussed) points to these "Many Worlds" are:

- Not Distant:

Unlike the "Cosmic Multiverse" (which posits distant bubble universes billions of lightyears away), this theory says the alternate worlds are right here, right now

- In Superposition:

They exist in the same space as you, but in a different "phase" or dimension of the wave function, much like radio stations occupying the same airwaves but on different frequencies.

- Sliding Doors:

Every time a quantum event has multiple possible outcomes, the universe splits. In one version, you catch the train; in another, you miss it. Both "yous" exist simultaneously in the same room but cannot see each other.

The Recent Finnish Research (The "Maths")

There are two recent major breakthroughs from Finland that fit this description. The first one is the most likely candidate for the "toy universe" idea:

Creating Universes on a Chip

Who: A team led by Professor Sorin Paraoanu at Aalto University.

The Discovery:

They used a quantum computer to create a "toy universe" inside the processor.

The Connection:

Instead of looking for distant universes, they mathematically simulated a universe with its own laws of physics (different from ours) inside the quantum chip. This proved that "universes" with alternate rules don't need to be far away—they can be created and observed" before you" in a lab.

A New Theory of Gravity

Who:

Researchers Mikko Partanen and Jukka Tulkki

The Discovery:

They published new mathematics proposing a Quantum Theory of Gravity that challenges the standard Big Bang model.

THE UNIVERSAL CONNECTION

Their math suggests we don't need "dark energy" or distant multiverses to explain the universe's expansion. It brings the explanation back to local, understandable quantum frames, potentially unifying the "micro" and "macro" worlds (a concept very aligned with The Sullivan Theory's Quan / Quanom structure).

Why this "Sliding Door Model" matters

This research scientifically backs The Sullivan Theory view that Quan (your personal reality) is the primary experience.

The Sullivan Theory's "Sliding Doors" model implies that by Observing, Orienting, Acting, Realising and Reflecting (the OOARR process), you are essentially "navigating" through the infinite spread of possible "Sliding Door" branches to experience the specific one you want, rather than creating it from scratch.

A radio is a useful analogy for the problems that many of us experience, our dial is stuck.

We unconsciously tune into the Anxious Navigator podcast frequencies every morning. We wake up, check our phone, remember our problems, and instantly lock onto "Anxiety Plus"

"The economy is crashing."

"I'm getting old."

"They don't respect me."

When you are tuned to these frequencies, you can only receive songs of stress and struggle. You can pray for peace, you can wish for wealth, but if your internal dial is set to "Lack," abundance cannot find you.

You do not need to change the universe (the Quantom). You need to change the frequency.

Who is turning the dial?

The Universe Through You

This is not a theoretical text. It is a practical guide.

The Quantom

This is the infinite ocean of potential.

It's the vast, distant and near cosmos, the field of all possibilities.

Your Quan

This is your own boat.

It is your personal, experienced universe—your health, your opportunities, your inner state, your relationships.

Right now, most of us create our Quan by default, unconsciously.

To steer your boat—your Quan—through the infinite ocean of the Quantom, you need to understand how the vessel actually works.

In the language of best selling author, Mel Robbins, the waves of the ocean are the "Let Them" field—these waves are going to exist, regardless of what you do.

Your personal reality is simply whatever waves happen to be surging around, under or crashing over your little boat.

This book seeks to help you create it consciously.

Let me be clear: this is not a manual for perfection.

Perfection doesn't create vitality; adaptation does.

80/20 Rhythm

True longevity and well-being aren't about maintaining a static, calm "balance."

Your cells don't seek balance—they seek rhythm.This is why a core principle of this book is the 80/20 Rhythm.

The "80%" is your conscious, coherent practice

—the time you spend using both your "oars" (AWE Awareness Wonder Expectancy and OOARR Observe Orient Act Realise Reflect) to intentionally create your personal universe.

The "20%" is... well, it's life

It's the "Let Them" field. It's the random interferences, the unexpected challenges, the waves that hit your boat.

Your Universal Boat - Your Quan

The boat metaphor for your Quan, your personal universe is pretty good. It helps remind us of the important elements of our existence.

The Hull: We can think of our Body/Health as the "Hull." If the hull is damaged (inflammation, lack of sleep), our boat will not be reliable, regardless of how good the oars are.

The Ocean: The Quantom, the universe of infinite possibilities.

Your Navigated Course : This is the result of your Observation, your Orientation (navigation), Your Action, your Realisation (navigation check), Your Reflection (ready to maintain or adjust course if your reflection reveals this is necessary)

THE MECHANICS OF CONSCIOUSNESS

Waking Up from the Drift

Neuroscience tells us we spend about 95% of our lives in a subconscious drift. We drive to work and don't remember the turns; we react to a partner's comment with a scripted defense mechanism; we reach for sugar not because we are hungry, but because we are bored.

This is Ambient Mode

In this mode, we are passive receivers of the infinite possibilities of the universe, the Quantom. We are like a device listening for a wake word (like Hey Siri, Hey Jade) that rarely comes.

In this state, the "Anxious Navigator"—that risk-averse, chattering part of the brain—is usually at the wheel. It loves Ambient Mode because it is safe, predictable, and reactive.

The "Chatter" is constant, narrating our fears and replaying our past, keeping us trapped in a loop of unconscious creation.

Most people live and die entirely in Ambient Mode, waiting for the world to happen to them.

Active Mode (The "Orient")

The moment of power—the spark of The Sullivan Theory—lies in the interruption.

In the near future, we will all have an AI companion. If we don't know how to Orient our personal universal consciousness , our Quan, our AI will help us calm and mediate our Anxious Navigator (C1-C2 Newtonian Trap). I already have a name for my personal AI. My middle name is Dermot. Some of my friends call me JD (for John Dermot). So my AI is called Jade.

Hey Jade, will you please narrate my book for me. Your voice sounds so much better than mine. At least my C1-C2 Newtonian Trap is telling me that.

Jade's response:

"Happy to do that Johnny!"

Before we can enlist AI to our crew, we must muster our Whole Brain Huddle, so you can lead your AI as an additional crew member, rather than letting it lead you.

The Orient is a physical and mental override. It is the moment you stop "listening" to the ambient noise of the world and the chatter of the Navigator, and you physically engage the "Wise

Visionary."

One day soon I may say "Hey Jade" to wake up Jade AI. I will always say "Hey Johnny" (which is what I call myself when I speak to myself out loud).

My beautiful, ever so gracious, long passed Mum, Pauline Terese Sullivan, always called me "Johnny". Mum used to sign her name P T Sullivan.

When we name ourselves out loud or call ourselves to attention in other ways, we are practicing the neurological act of Metacognition (thinking about our thinking).

We are moving from passenger to pilot.

- Ambient Mode is the drift. It is "Letting it happen."
- Active Mode is the creation. It is "Making it happen."

The goal is not to eliminate Ambient Mode—we need it to function.

The goal is to increase the frequency of the Orient

Every time you consciously interrupt the drift to Orient your compass, you reclaim a piece of your personal universe, your wonderful Quan. You prove to the Universe that you are awake at the oars.

The practice is not to eliminate the 20%.

It is about using the Orient and Reflect steps to handle it, integrate it, learn from it, and as often as you can, consciously, come back to your 80% rhythm.

In the pages that follow, we will first explore these patterns through real stories, to give you comfort and context.

Then, we will walk step-by-step through the practical tools to master your 80% practice.

The journey from a purely reactive human to a conscious creator is the most important journey you will ever take. You just have to be willing to pick up your oars.

Let's continue.

A TALE OF TWO STATES

You will recall I opened this book with this famous quote from Charles Dickens'

"A Tale of Two Cities"

Well Dickens book could also have been titled "A Tale of Two States" (Quantum States)

I will bring it into Quantum play. When it "occurred to me" it was very much that "Aha" moment that Sir Roger Penrose speaks of. I was heading down to the first tee at Margaret River Golf Course and I laughed out loud and had to explain to a guy on the 10th tee that I was laughing at something funny rather than him. I raced after Marg and mentioned this and Charles Dickens. Who knows, in a quantum powered universe of infinite possibilities I can imagine the consciousness of Charles Dickens was communicating with me. I said to Marg that, if this was the case, Charles would have a fresh insight into the Quantum potentials of his opening line.

In physics, superposition is the ability of a quantum system to be in multiple states at the same time until it is measured. Dickens creates a perfect literary equivalent of this paradox, holding two contradictory states of reality in suspension simultaneously.

Here is how Dickens' "Quantum Narrative" breaks down:

The Superposition of 1775

Dickens doesn't say "It was a good time for some and a bad time for others."

This is the alternative / multiworld phrasing that Charles could have run with. This was the idea that made me laugh out loud on the golf course.

Dickens asserts that the time itself existed in both states at once.

An aside for those interested in quantum physics: If we were to write the "Dickens State" notation, it might look like this :

For those listening via audiobook just hang in there for a minute. You never know you may be intrigued.

So in mathematical expression, The State Vector of the Time of A Tale of Two Cities (circa 1775, the time of The French Revolution) is equal to one over the square root of two, multiplied by the superposition of the Best of Times State and the Worst of Times State.

This represents the reality of the situation at that time. One over the square root of two is the probability amplitude. It ensures that if you square it (to find the probability), you get 1/2 (or 50%) for each outcome.

The Plus Sign does not mean "add" in the normal sense. It means "and." Both states exist simultaneously in suspension.

In Quantum Mechanics, the special bracket is called a Ket. It acts like a container or a bucket that holds a specific state of reality. When you see a Ket at the end, it signifies that the description of that quantum state is complete.

Just like Schrödinger's cat is both alive and dead until the box is opened, the era of the French Revolution held the potential for arguably the greatest human liberation and the greatest human cruelty simultaneously.

THE OBSERVER EFFECT

In quantum mechanics, the wave function collapses when an observer measures it. In "A Tale of Two Cities", the "collapse" happens through the specific characters:

For Charles Darnay: The reality collapses into "The Worst of Times" (imprisonment, threat of execution).

For Sydney Carton: It eventually collapses into "The Best of Times" (redemption and a "far, far better thing").

By holding these opposites together in that opening paragraph (Wisdom/Foolishness, Belief/Incredulity, Light/Darkness), Dickens forces the reader to accept a non-binary reality—a very quantum way of viewing history.

PART 2: THE PROCESS

Your Two Oars: AWE Awareness Wonder Expectancy and OOARR Observe Orient Act Realise Reflect

To begin this journey, you need to become intimately aware of the key input : outputs (IO) for creation of your personal universe.

AWE (Awareness, Wonder, Expectancy)

This is your internal state.

It's the "input" for creation, the way you tune your consciousness.

OOARR (Observe, Orient, Act, Realise, Reflect)

This is the active 5-stage loop.

It's the "process" you use to manifest your intentions in the real world.

Now, this is the happy design: AWE (A W E) and OOARR (O O A R R) are pronounced exactly the same way.

It's a single syllable, and the sound is just like the "oar" of a boat.

Remembering to use both your oars each day will help you remember and apply to the entire process.

Just like a boat's oars, AWE (A W E) and OOARR (O O A R R) are wonderful oars for giving your life direction.

When you feel powerless, you are like a boat being pushed around by the currents of misunderstandings and the waves of misfortune.

By consciously using the "oars" of AWE (Awareness Wonder Expectancy as your internal state) and OOARR (Observe Orient Act Realise Reflect as your active process), you are no longer at the mercy of the current. You gain the power to steer, to overcome resistance, and to intentionally move in the direction you choose.

THE NEWTONIAN TRAP

Here is why you are exhausted.

In a life lived by default, the Primal Alarm (C2) part of our brain sees a threat—say, a criticism at work or from your partner or a family member or a friend. It screams,

"We are under attack!"

Instead of checking with the Lookout, also known as the Sensory Anchor (C3) and the Captain, also known as C4, the Wise Visionary, who are the vital right side crew we have in our brain: the Navigator (C1) becomes very nervous in response to the Primal Alarm (C2) and jumps in to "fix" the anxious, "what if", or neurotic, "what is" feelings sharply changing course based on what "appears" like logic.

The Navigator starts rehearsing a defensive mental conversation. It argues (to you) all the reasons they are wrong and you are right.

This is the C2-C1 Loop.

As I call it, the Newtonian Trap.

You are using the aggressive energy of the Navigator to try to solve the panic of the Alarm. It creates a closed loop of high-voltage static, potentially even an out of control electrical fire.

The more you think (C1), the more you validate the danger, and the louder the Alarm (C2) screams.

The Captain (C4) has dropped his oars and The Lookout (C3) is drowned out by the Alarm (C2) and the Navigator, C1's chatter. Your little boat, your precious Quan, is being thrashed by the waves.

THE SOLUTION: THE WHOLE BRAIN HUDDLE

We are not trying to throw the Navigator overboard. We need the Navigator to navigate our course and avoid the storms, if possible, and always avoid the rocks. We need the Alarm to warn us of actual storms.

The goal is not silence; the goal is Coherence.

We need to call a Whole Brain Huddle, a crew meeting.

Imagine the crew gathering in your little boat:

First off, as you would expect, The Alarm (C2) reports the threat:

"The waves are getting high!"

The Lookout, who is also responsible for the Anchor, The Sensory Anchor (C3) checks reality:

"We are wet, but the boat is holding. The water is actually refreshing."

The Captain, The Wise Visionary (C4) sees the wave:

"We are safe. Let's adjust the oars and ride this wave rather than fighting it."

The Navigator (C1) sets the course: "Understood. Let's adjust course now."

When you move from the Newtonian Trap to the Huddle, you stop reacting to the universe's infinite, random, sometimes dissonant Quantom of frequencies and start resonating with it.

To call this Huddle, you need a signal strong enough to break the panic of the Newtonian Trap. You need a safe word.

Your safe word is "awe".

THE TYRANNY OF THE "DEFAULT"

As you may have gathered already and as we will explore more, this "Nervous Navigator" is the voice of two characters in your left brain. Here we are drawing on the personal experiences and groundbreaking research of Harvard's Dr. Jill Bolte Taylor.

When, in 2025, I heard Jill in an interview with globally renowned international podcaster, Steven Bartlett, who asked her,(as she recounted the story of her hemorrhagic stroke, which shut down the left hemisphere of her brain and left her with loss of all left brain function and with a recovery path of 8 years), "What is the complex range of emotions you're experiencing as you recount this story?"

Jill voiced the word "Awe," I nearly burst into tears.

"Oh, I feel such awe for life... life .. this is life... this is life .... and there is death .. and we have life and life is the miracle construction of the universe. Argue about it all you want. Have a million conversations about it. Analyze it to death..

Straight back to the part of my brain, that right thinking part that connects me in that transformation .. or that trans .. transcendence experience..

Of being so much more than just a little human being running around the planet.

Oh my gosh! Life is this miracle and it makes me feel awe and wonder ..

It excites me so !"

That word—

awe

- so foundational to everything I had been contemplating and writing—was another profound confirmation.

Dr. Bolte Taylor's work gives us the practical language for these inner characters, "those parts of the brain" Jill talks about.

We have already come to know our left-brain characters as our Primal Alarm C1 and our Navigator C2. And, just as importantly, we will learn to connect with our right-brain characters: the present-moment Sensory Anchor C3 and the creative Wise Visionary C4.

We also know that the "Nervous Navigator" voice comes from C1 and C2 having control of our boat and, effectively, our personal universe, our Quan.

Their job is to manage your sense of "self" by constantly running your past (regrets, memories) and your future (plans, worries).

It's the voice of "me, my, and mine."

While it's essential for navigating the world, it has one critical side effect: It locks us into our past. It creates our reality by re-running old programs.

When these two characters are in charge, you aren't creating your life; you are defaulting to it.

This default state is your unconsciously created, personal, experienced universe -to name this universe to better understand it and be aware of it.

This is your little boat - your drifting (unconscious) Quan— your boat, possibly as it currently exists, built from the sum of your past beliefs, habits, and reactions.

We also know that the "Nervous Navigator" voice comes from C1 and C2 having control of our boat and, effectively, our personal universe, our Quan.

Vitally, we will learn to connect with our right-brain characters: the present-moment Sensory Anchor C3 and the creative Wise Visionary C4.

Gazing at the ocean or the starry sky, the act of getting lost in music— these are examples of connection to the all-encompassing, conscious energy of the universe - the Quantom - the field of infinite potential from which all realities emerge.

The problem is, we spend most of our time stuck in our unconscious Quan, listening to the default chatter of our left-brain characters, completely unaware of the infinite Quantom potential available to us in every second.

The Great Promise

What if you could change that?

What if that feeling of awe wasn't an accident, but a companion?

What if you could learn to quiet the "Nervous Navigator" at will, not just when you're at the beach, but when you're in traffic, in a difficult meeting, or simply sitting on your couch?

This book is built on a simple, radical promise: You can.

The experience of awe, as the research confirms, engages your whole brain, but it often begins on the right side—the home of your Anchor C3 and Visionary C4. It is the perfect neurological antidote to the narrow, past-focused chatter of your C1 and C2.

You can learn to shift your consciousness. You can move from being a passive reactor to your life to being its conscious, intentional co-creator

It all begins with the state of AWE.

AWE: THE STATE OF CONSCIOUS CREATION

I was discussing this very chapter with our friends Peter and Natalia that mid November 2025 night. Peter made a very good point. Peter was concerned that by turning "awe"—such a deep, powerful, and profound emotion—into an acronym, we might diminish it.

It's a critical point, but this framework is designed to do the exact opposite.

Let's consider fractals.

A fractal pattern is described as something that "repeats at every level," from the grandest scale (like the view of Earth from space) to the smallest, everyday experiences.

I was discussing this very chapter with our friends Peter and Natalia one mid November 2025 evening over dinner in Margaret River. Peter made a very good point. He was concerned that by turning "awe"—such a deep, powerful, and profound emotion—into an acronym, we might diminish it.

It's a critical point, but this framework is designed to do the exact opposite.

Let's consider fractals. A fractal pattern is described as something that "repeats at every level," from the grandest scale (like the view of Earth from space) to the smallest, everyday experiences.

Peter mentioned the 2024 Booker Prize-winning novella, "Orbital" which is set with such views from the international space station and considers the impact of the experience of awe on the characters and experiences .

Let's try to imagine the impact of the grandest real fractal of awe humans have experienced so far: the view of Earth from space.

Imagine the perspective of those 12 astronauts who have stood on the moon and looked back at our entire, fragile, glowing world.

A total of 24 humans have viewed the Earth from the Moon.

These men were all NASA astronauts who traveled to the Moon during the Apollo program between 1968 and 1972. No humans have returned to the Moon's vicinity since. Although that is likely to change soon.

Here is the breakdown of those 24 individuals:

12 Astronauts walked on the lunar surface and viewed Earth from the ground.

12 Astronauts orbited the Moon (or flew around it, in the

case of Apollo 13) without landing, viewing Earth from their spacecraft.

Three men made the journey twice: Jim Lovell (Apollo 8 & 13), John Young (Apollo 10 & 16), and Gene Cernan (Apollo 10 & 17).

Because they are counted as unique individuals, the total remains 24.

The View: While all 24 saw Earth from the Moon's vicinity, the most famous image of this perspective, "Earthrise," was taken by Bill Anders during the Apollo 8 mission—the first time humans ever orbited the Moon.

The wonderful news for our own personal experiences of awe is that fractal patterns repeat at every level. We can look at the moon and the stars with awe as well. We can behold a fractal of the universe of awe in an oceanside rockpool.

The AWE framework isn't just for 'exceptional' moments. It's for the 'small' fractals. AWE trains us to find that same profound connection in the everyday.

This is where this way of thinking expands awe, potentially infinitely.

The Awareness, Wonder, Expectancy, the emotion of awe, can be felt beholding an orchid, an ant, or a butterfly; listening to the wind, a bird singing its morning song.

Awe is a fractal emotion. It scales.

Peter also mentioned Julia Baird's beautiful book,

Phosphorescence, which was inspired by her own awe at that magical, glittering light in the water. That is a fractal of awe.

You can feel it in the vital beating of your own heart, or the conscious miracle of your next breath.

Awe is not diminished; it is amplified and woven into the fabric of your everyday life.

So, in this book, AWE is both the profound emotion and the practical protocol for "tuning" your consciousness to connect with the Quantom - the field of infinite potential from which all realities emerge.

Awe is the "input" desired so you can consciously create.

The AWE acronym points to a three-part process:

Awareness: This is the "small self" moment you feel at the ocean. It is the scientific antidote to the Default Mode. It is the act of recognizing the infinite potential of the Quantom and the chatter of your "Nervous Navigator" for what it is—just one voice, not you.

Wonder: This is the "mind-blown" feeling of awe. When you encounter true vastness, your old mental models must stretch. This is the state of profound, non-judgmental curiosity. It's the moment you stop assuming your old beliefs are true and ask, "What else is possible?"

Expectancies: This is where you move from passive observer to active participant. From a state of Awareness and Wonder, you apply focused, intentional belief to "select" a potential from the Quantom, beginning the sacred process of drawing it into your personal reality.

Stuck in Traffic : Now or in the Future

Let's skip ahead just a little in our wonderful Quan boat adventure story

We are going to consider some very significant life, global and universal examples deeper into this book.

For now let's consider a seemingly trivial example: You are stuck in heavy traffic.

Even with (seemingly) trivial situations we should never ignore our boat (us) in distress. Things can get out of control very quickly in life and so often do.

So this is how to mount a rescue mission.

Here is how to apply our AWE (Awareness Wonder Expectancy) and OOARR (Observe, Orient, Act, Realise, Reflect) framework to break both the Neurotic and Anxious Navigator loops, to a stuck in traffic scenario.

The goal in both cases is to stop the Navigator from spinning in a Left Brain only closed circuit and reconnect yourself to the wider reality/Right Brain (the infinite universe of possibilities, the Quantom) so, consciously, you can stabilise your personal universe, your Quan.

BREAKING THE NEUROTIC NAVIGATOR LOOP (THE CONTROL TRAP)

Context: You are frustrated because reality (the traffic in this case) is not following your plan (to get from A to B quickly).

How is AWE possible for me in heavy traffic?

Awareness:

Become aware of your internal dialogue of "shoulds."

Check:

"Am I angry because something is actually dangerous, or because it is just "different" from what I wanted?"

Move from Judgment to Wonder.

Instead of "This is stupid!"

Ask, "I wonder what this disruption is trying to teach me?"

There is a better Expectancy

"I wonder how I can use this unexpected event?"

O - Observe (Step Back and Pause)

The Shift:

Notice the physical tension (jaw, fists).

Label it: "This is a Neurotic Loop. I am resisting reality."

O - Orient (Re-Align)

Shift from Resistance to Adaptation.

New Thought:

"My navigation was wrong. Let's get better directions. Let's check Waze and possibly find a better route. "

A - Act (Move Forward)

The Action:

Do the most constructive thing possible with the "current reality", not the one you wished for.

The Strategy:

With this trivial example: you are stuck in traffic.

The "Neurotic Act" is honking and fuming.

This has been known to escalate into road rage if someone pushes in.

Examples of awe inspiration include putting on an audiobook , practicing breathing or both. Appreciating the moment.

R - Realise (Manifestation)

The Outcome:

Witness the immediate result of your acceptance.

Notice that the situation feels lighter because you stopped adding the weight of your resistance to it.

The Evidence: You navigated the disruption without burning energy on anger.

R - Reflect (Integration)

The Lesson

"My Primal Alarm and Navigator parts of me caused the pain, not the event itself."

The Upgrade:

Update the Navigator's and Primal Alarm's hard drives :

Flexibility is a higher form of control than rigidity. Check in with your senses. See the world with AWE.

Breaking the Anxious Navigator Loop (The Fear Trap)

Context: You are anxious about a hypothetical future issue (heavy traffic)

Seek AWE (Awareness Wonder Expectancy)

Awareness of your internal dialogue of "What if."

The Check:

"Am I solving a problem that exists right now, or am I writing a horror movie about traffic next Tuesday?"

The Shift:

Label it: "This is an Anxious Loop. I am time-travelling."

Wonder about something wonderful, it's easy if you try.

Have an Expectancy for light traffic next Tuesday.

SELF-AWE: THE FOUNDATION FOR CHANGE

The "Brain Pivot" from reaction to creation is only possible if you have first done the work of Self AWE.

This is the act of turning the AWE lens inward. It is the prerequisite for all conscious creation.

Self-Awareness (The 'A')

This is the vital, non-negotiable first step.

It is the process of taking a deep, honest, and non-judgmental inventory of your "givens"—the complete 80/20 of your life.

A Personal Note on Self-Awareness This practice is not an intellectual exercise for me. My personal "Self-Awareness" inventory includes:

A lifelong, close relationship with schizophrenia, which was an unimaginable life challenge for my beautiful, loving and gracious Mum, for all my childhood through to my twenties. Mum had increasingly less major episodes later in life as she unconsciously put herself on a keto diet, simply through her inclination to eat less and skip meals (recently this has been discovered to have major beneficial impacts on schizophrenia) .

My dear Dad suffered from very severe, debilitating PTSD and consequent alcoholism from his service in WWII, fighting in the jungle of Bougainville.

I came to a moment of awareness about the "reasonableness" of my Dad's state of mind in my early thirties, when he was in his early sixties and had moderated his drinking and his anger had submerged, when I watched an ABC Australia interview with a courageous nurse who served in the Vietnam War. She was asked how she was at that time and she responded with words to the effect:

"I am angry and alcoholic!"

The interviewer looked surprised.

The nurse sensed his surprise and added words to the effect:

"Everyone is, unless you're a psychopath!"

The Department of Veterans Affairs in Australia did not provide an assessment of Dad's total and permanent disability until his mid-fifties, more than thirty years after the war.

The combination of Dad's state of physical and mental health, with Mum's mental health was that our family lived in comparative lack through 1960s and 70s Australia.

I remember putting cardboard in my shoes to patch over the holes in the soles. I also darned my socks until they didn't fit me.

In 1975 I was captain of my school. I remember being invited along to meet the Governor of New South Wales, Sir Roden Cutler at the Governor's House, overlooking the Opera House and Sydney Harbour.. All those there were wearing their school jackets, except me. Sir Roden's aide-de-camp came over to me and asked where my jacket was. He found a jacket for me but it had no buttons.

As I approached Sir Roden and Lady Cutler, in the line up of others, I was holding the jacket tight so it looked buttoned up like all the others. As I extended my hand to shake hands with Sir Roden, my jacket flew open. I was supposed to say:

"Your Excellency" and nod to Lady Cutler "Lady Cutler"

Instead I said: "Howyagoin' mate!"

Sir Roden, who was a Victoria Cross winner, laughed out loud. He came over to me especially at morning tea and spent time talking with me. A lovely man.

I also remember I became a pretty good forger. I had to artistically modify out of date train passes to get to school by train. I used to press through with the crowd to minimise the time the ticket guy at the station would have to cast his eyes over the pass. I can recall being anxious from time to time when ticket inspectors would come by and have a close look. I was a pretty good artist. Not as good as my Dad

Sadly Dad's talent was never realised and all his great sketch art was destroyed by either him or Mum. I suspect by Mum as I recall her smashing a spectacular pretty large scale photo of Mum and Dad on their wedding day. I have no doubt it was paid for by her Dad, my Pa. She did not smash the second large scale wedding photo with just her. They were such a beautiful couple.

Childhood Trauma

Ever-present anxiety about whether our Dad would arrive home drunk and enraged.

Fear and awe when mum was experiencing psychotic episodes, largely centred around seeing the devil.

The Self-AWE process allows me now to look at these givens and others with non-judgmental clarity and move to the next step: Self-Wonder.

Self-Wonder (The 'W')

Once you have this non-judgmental list, you apply Self-Wonder. This is the antidote to your inner critic.

Applying Self-Wonder to My Story Instead of judging my inventory, I learned to get curious about it.

"I wonder if this genetic potential for 'schizophrenia'—this unique brain wiring—is also the very source of my creativity and ability to see the patterns that became this theory?"

"I wonder if navigating my father's severe trauma is what gave me a profound capacity for resilience and empathy?"

"I wonder if my 'poor' upbringing is the source of my resourcefulness and my deep, fundamental drive to create a life of purpose?"

Self-Wonder reframes your 20% "givens" from a life sentence to the raw material of your 80% practice.

Self-Expectancy (The 'E')

This is the final, active step. It is the act of applying focused, loving belief to yourself.

"I expect that I can adapt"

"I expect that I can learn and grow from my past"

"I expect that I have the power to manage my 80% to create a coherent personal universe, consciously created Quan, from this very raw material."

THE ANTIDOTE TO OUR "DEFAULT"

Why is this state of AWE so critical? Because it is the direct antidote to the modern epidemic of alienation, isolation, loneliness, and cynicism. It is the experience of a double rainbow cutting through a grey sky.

The "Nervous Navigator"—our left-brain C1 and C2—operates on the "fight or flight" sympathetic nervous system. It's a state of tension, contraction, and self-focus.

This is where we find a critical tension, because fear and awe often go together. Awe is what you feel beholding a powerful lightning strike from a safe distance; fear is what you feel when it crashes right outside your window. Fear dampens awe. Physiologically, this is the amygdala (our fear alarm) activating and suppressing the vagus nerve (our calm-and-connect system).

When we can experience vastness without that threat, or when our sense of wonder is stronger than our fear, true awe takes over. It fully activates the vagus nerve, which is the physiological antithesis of fight or flight. It's what slows us down. It's the source of those goosebumps you feel, the trigger for oxytocin (the "connection" hormone) to be released. It is, in physical form, that oceanic sense of being part of something larger than yourself.

When this happens, two crucial things occur in your brain:

It deactivates the amygdala, your brain's fear and anxiety alarm.

It deactivates the Default Mode Network, the part that hosts the "Nervous Navigator's" self-focused chatter.

Awe, in short, gets you out of your own head.

The Universal Triggers

Dr. Keltner's team has studied awe across more than 30 countries, and the triggers are beautifully universal.

We find it in nature. Imagine Charles Darwin on the shores of the Galápagos. Darwin would have spent a vast amount of his time in a state of pure, observational awe, which is precisely what allowed him to see the profound patterns no one else had seen.

Keltner mentions that awe may be found among nature too. Think of Jane Goodall's profound observation of gorillas watching, completely absorbed, in the powerful display of a waterfall. His research reveals, many find it in music. Yumi Kendall, a cellist, whom Dacher interviewed and studied for his research, is not just playing her instrument; she is filled with awe by the sound and feeling she is co-creating.

We find it in moral beauty—witnessing an act of profound courage or kindness.

We find it in the great cycles of life and death. I watched my father die. I looked at him dead, and I was in awe of the sheer, profound finality of it.

I said to him, "You're dead, mate."

It was darkly comedic.

In that observation, I was not afraid of death. I am not afraid of death at all.

The observation was a process, a transition, a moment of ultimate perspective. In my next book, which has a working title:

"The Source, The Code, Infinity and The Universal Interface"

I imagine orienting to one of those multiple worlds, which happens to be called death by us, possibly moving from analog to digital. Who knows.

THE PRACTICE OF AWE

In any event I hope to be in a state of Awareness, Wonder, Expectancy.

Awe as a state is our birthright. I believe children experience awe far more than adults. It is a state we can return to.

The consistent thread, from every culture, is the same. In the face of awe, your sense of self becomes small, and your sense of connection becomes large. "Myself isn't that important," is the universal feeling.

This is why Dacher Keltner sees awe as a future part of

healthcare, a potent treatment for conditions like PTSD. The experience of awe is a powerful reset.

How do we get it? While some look to psychedelics or VR, I believe the most sustainable and powerful sources are all around us: nature, music, sports, literature, art, and relationships.

Dr. Keltner talks about scheduling "awe," perhaps for 10 minutes each week, to look for it.

My view is that experiencing awe should be everyday.

It should be in the morning, at the ocean or just with your own breath. It should be at night, with the night sky. After all, before we had roofs over our heads and kitchens inside, humans would be out by the fire, beholding that expansive, universe-connecting night sky.

We must shift from defaulting to our unconscious Quan to intentionally seeking AWE, seeking awe as the new morning light and evening light markers for our day, turbo charging conscious creation of our personal universe - our Quan.

This book is built on a simple premise: The universe does not have to happen to you; it can happen through you.

From this grounded, scientifically-backed state of Awareness, Wonder, and Expectancy, we are ready to begin the process of creation. We are ready to Observe, Orient, Act, Realise and Reflect.

YOU ARE A CREATOR, NOT A REACTOR

We all have moments—maybe even entire days or weeks—where we feel like we are simply reacting to life. We react to a social media post, a misleading text, or the deep pain of gaslighting from someone we love. We see how their reactions escalate, spreading into widespread gossip, and before we know it, we're hearing untruths and innuendo about ourselves from people we know and love and from people we don't even know.

Many of us, including me for most of my life, operated in what I now consider as the Newtonian world. For every action there is an equal and opposite reaction.

We Observe then We React.

This "reactor" state is exhausting. It leaves us feeling powerless, like we are being tossed around by forces outside of our control.

The Trap of One-Dimensional Contact

Part of this 'reactor' problem is the depth of our communication. Texts, social posts, and emails are fundamentally one-dimensional. They are flat. They are breeding grounds for misunderstanding, disconnection, and reaction.

As creators, we choose another path. We seek deeper, richer connections.

We know that meeting in person is best, but we also use technology wisely. A video call carries so much more truth and connection than a simple audio call, and soon we'll likely be doing this with holograms.

The purpose of this book is to give you the tools to move from reacting to these flat, one-dimensional attacks to consciously creating a rich, multi-dimensional world. You are, in every moment, the conscious creator of your personal universe.

THE CREATION LOOP OBSERVATION: THE FIRST ACT OF CREATION

This state of AWE is the key that unlocks the door.

How do you walk through the door which takes you to your new and better world?

You continue with the next step of the active process of

conscious creation: Observation.

You cannot change what you do not see.

If you try to observe your life from your "default mode," you will only see your old stories, your justifications, and your limitations.

To truly Observe—to see your unconscious personal universe as it is.

Throughout this book, we will journey together through this entire process.

You will learn not only to Observe, but to Orient your internal state, to take inspired Action, to Realise new possibilities in the present moment, and to Reflect on the new reality you are creating.

OOARR is a fractal process and an infinite loop, extending before and beyond lifetimes.

OOARR can occur in an instant, from Observation, Orientation, Action, Realisation, Reflection (with Reflection returning us instantly to Re-Observation, Re-orientation, Action (not reaction), Realisation, Reflection.

You will discover that once you have engaged AWE to quiet the "Nervous Navigator" and step out of your default programming. You have opened your senses. You are now in the clear, potent state of Observation.

For the first time, perhaps, you can see your personal universe —your unconscious Quan—with true clarity, without the fog of old judgments.

More importantly, you have stood at the shore of your own mind.

You have glimpsed that vast ocean of infinite potential, the

Quantom, and you are no longer just an observer, but a participant.

You can see what is: You can sense what could be.

This brings you to the most pivotal moment in conscious creation.

A vast field of possibilities lies before you.

The "Nervous Navigator" (your C1 - C2 loop) is quiet, but it hasn't disappeared.

Your creative, right-brain characters (your C3 and C4) are present and waiting.

Now... which way do you face?

This is not a passive choice. It is the second and most crucial step of the OOARR process. It is the act of Orientation.

To Orient is to align your internal state—your thoughts, feelings, and beliefs—with the multiple potentials, multiple goals, you wish to draw from those sliding door moments before you.

It is the internal compass setting before you take a single step.

You have oriented in a direction. Now, you must choose your destination.

The journey from a purely reactive human to a conscious creator is the most important journey you will ever take. Let's continue this process.

PART 3 : ORIENTATION

TUNING YOUR CONSCIOUSNESS & UNDERSTANDING THE LOOP

Two Universes: Quantom and Quan

Before we can explore your personal universe, it will help to understand where your personal universe fits..When you look up at the night sky, you see the vast, shared reality we all perceive. Beneath this visible world, underlying all of it, is an infinite, invisible field. This field is not empty; it is pure, unformed potential. It is the "is-ness" of all things, the source from which every star, every planet, every cell, and every possible experience emerges.

As I have mentioned, I call this all-encompassing, potential energy of the many worlds before you, the Quantom. The Quantom is not just empty, random "stuff." It is a dynamic ocean of potential. It contains the blueprint for everything that has been, is, or ever could be - the "Many Worlds" / Sliding Doors possibilities. It encapsulates the "Let Them" field which best selling author Mel Robbins speaks and writes about.

You cannot control the Quantom, any more than a single drop of water can control the entire ocean. You are not separate from it. You are a unique consciousness within this ocean of consciousness..

Every single thing you could ever want, be, or experience — including improved, potentially vibrant health, creative insights, new opportunities, feelings of peace—already exist as potentials, as wave frequencies, within the Quantom.

This is a potentially profound and scientifically resonant refinement of our understanding of the universe. By viewing the Quantom not just as a "field" but as an infinite spectrum of waves bridges the gap between the physics of the Quantum and the metaphysics of Om.

In this model, reality is not initially "solid"; it is vibrational.

The Science of the Spectrum

These thoughts align with Quantum Field Theory (QFT).

In modern physics, there are no truly solid "particles" in the way we classically imagine them.

Instead, the universe is filled with fields—fluid-like substances spread throughout space.

What we perceive as a particle (an electron, a photon) is actually a wave or a ripple moving through that field.

•

The Quantom:

The sum total of all these fields and their potential vibrations.

It is the "hum" of infinite possibility before a signal is selected.

The Om (Vibration):

Since sound is vibration, the "Om" in Quantom represents the fundamental frequency or "hum" of existence.

The Implication: You are a Tuner

If the Quantom is an infinite spectrum of waves (like the entire radio spectrum), then your Consciousness is the receiver.

The personal, living process:

Let Them (The Quantom)

The waves exist.

All possibilities (joy, struggle, wealth, peace) are currently broadcasting on different frequencies.

You do not need to "create" the wave; the wave is already there.

Let Me (The Quan)

You cannot experience the entire spectrum at once (just as a radio cannot play every station at once).

You must tune into a specific bandwidth.

Your Quan is simply the frequency you are currently resonating with.

Applying this Wave Theory to your input AWE (Awareness Wonder Expectancy) and output OOARR (Observe, Orient, Act, Realise, Reflect) this Wave Theory clarifies the mechanics of the dual "oars" Algorithm:

AWE (The Tuning Dial)

Awareness: Acknowledging that the spectrum is infinite.

Wonder: Scanning the frequencies without judgment.

Expectancy: Locking into a specific frequency which encompasses a multitude of coherent waves (for example, "I expect to find 'Healing and Vitality, starting with John's very sore back").

OOARR (The Signal Processing)

Observe:

What wave am I currently tuned to?

Is my reality static and heavy, or light and fluid?

Orient:

Adjusting your internal vibration to match the wave you want to receive.

You cannot catch a "Healing" wave if your internal receiver is set to "Doubt."

Act:

The physical movement that collapses that wave into matter (collapsing the wave function).

The Wave Model Concepts

The Wave Analogy : The Sullivan Theory

The Universe - The infinite spectrum of all waves - which I have called The Quantom

You : The Receiver of your unique universal Consciousness

Your Reality : The specific station playing right now : Your personal, conscious or unconscious, universe - your Quan

The Process : Turning the dial to a clear signal with AWE (Awareness Wonder Expectancy) and with OOARR (Observe Orient Act Realise Reflect)

Your Mind Is a Frequency Tuner, Not just a Manifestation Tool

Your mind functions more like a frequency tuner selecting a reality from a field of waves, rather than a biological tool that creates something out of nothing.

The question, then, is how do you tune it?

If the Quantom is the infinite spectra of all potential, Quan is what you personally experience within it.

It is the portion of the infinite universe, the Quantom, that you have materialized—consciously or unconsciously—through your unique focus, beliefs, and actions.

Let's consider a personal case of where the materiality of the world meets and try to challenge this theory.

This is the ultimate stress test for any metaphysical theory. If a philosophy cannot account for the brute force of my back spasms as I write this, then the theory is just a daydream.

If Consciousness precedes Materiality, why is Materiality , my current (at the time of writing this, severe QL spasms in my lower back, trying to dictate my entire Consciousness?

Here is how we refine The Sullivan Theory to survive the collision with physical pain.

THE MATERIAL WORLD IS OUR QUANTUM "SOUNDING BOARD"

Materiality is not "The Enemy"—It is the "Sounding Board"

In contemplating this, I said to myself:

"If you didn't 'feel' materiality this would be death."

Exactly. In the Quantom (the infinite void), there is no friction, no gravity, and no pain.

There may or may not be experience, at least as we understand experience.

Although I have to say, I am hoping the transition from life to afterlife will be like going from analog to digital.

Can you "play" the universe without an instrument? Maybe, but we don't know.

So, for the time being, our bodies are the instrument.

The Theory Refined : Consciousness precedes Materiality in origin, but Materiality constrains Consciousness in experience.

The Analogy : Think of a guitar string. If the string is loose (no tension/materiality), you can pluck it all you want with your consciousness, but it makes no sound. It requires Tension to create a Note.

The Application : My QL injury is currently under "Extreme Tension." The note it is playing is loud and discordant (Pain). The fact that I feel it proves I am fully engaged with the interface of life. Numbness would mean the connection is severed.

The "Feedback Loop" Function

If your mind is the Tuner, then the body (Materiality) is the Feedback Mechanism.

In the image I provide in the book here, you see where our QL muscles sit. They anchor the rib cage (breath) to the pelvis (movement) and the spine (structure). So healthy QLs are very critical for the healthy operation of our body.

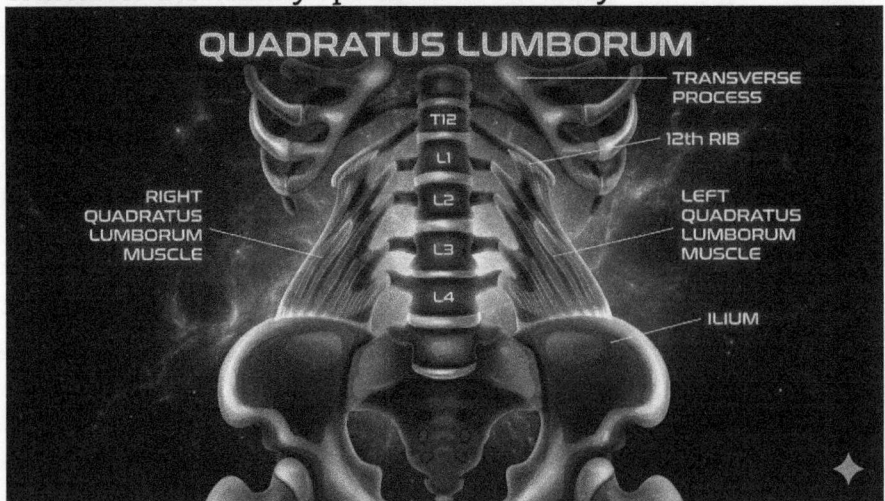

An aside here: Many people have heard about the 33 vertebrae in their spine, including the 5 Lumbar vertebrae L1, L2, L3, L4, L5 at the base of their spine, in proximity to where our QL muscles are located. Also, the 7 Cervical Vertebrae in our neck (C1 to C7). Everyone will know how critical these C1 to C7 are for living.

However, I am sure that most of you will have never heard of our C1, C2, C3, and C4 in our brain. These are not bones (but if it helps you to remember, think of bonehead. You will come to appreciate why this mnemonic is especially relevant to those of us stuck in our thinking)

These four crew members of our brains are at least as important if not more important than the crew members which make up our spine (we know what happens if we disconnect any of these). You will learn a lot more about our brain's C1-C4 very soon.

Back to my QL and consciously creating my reality.

When you "tune" your reality, you don't just tune it in a vacuum. You tune it through the medium of the body.

The Signal: I went for a swim (Conscious intent: Health, Vitality). I had my daily swim, enjoyed Balance (a combo of Tai Chi, Yoga and Pilates), including my daily handstand, and played golf the day before. Not unusual but it seems I injured myself.

The Feedback : The QL spasmed in the change room and got progressively worse yesterday morning and today as I write this.

The Meaning : This isn't a failure of creation. It is High-Fidelity Feedback. The material world is shouting back at the tuner:

"The frequency you are trying to run (Physical Exertion) is currently incompatible with the hardware's capacity."

If I didn't feel the pain, I would have kept on moving until my QL muscle ripped off the bone. The pain is the Materiality protecting my mind-body which processes my Consciousness.

Reconciling "The Tuner" with "The Spasm"

So, how do we apply the "Mind as Tuner" when the dial is stuck on "Pain"?

We have to differentiate between The Carrier Wave and The Program.

The Carrier Wave (Materiality) : This is the raw sensation. The electrical signals shooting up your spine. This is undeniable. You cannot "tune" this out completely without drugs or dissociation. This proves you are alive.

The Program (Consciousness) : This is the information you decode from that wave.

Default Process :

"This is bad. I am broken. This ruins my week." (This adds suffering to the pain).

AWE PROCESS

"This is a proximity alarm. My body is demanding stillness. I am experiencing intense sensation in the lower quadrant."

The Challenge to the Theory

Does my consciousness create this pain?

My Theory answers : No. My consciousness created the conditions (the swim, the lifestyle), and the Materiality (physics/biology) responded with a limit.

The Real Power :

The "God-moment" in this theory is that it is not magically healing the back instantly.

It is the ability to feel the weight of Materiality (the spasm, the genetics, market histrionics, where you live) and not let that weight (or weights) collapse your Observe/Orient loop.

I am proving the theory right now by sitting here, experiencing strong pain over the last two days, and engaging in high-level philosophy and science.

My Materiality, my body, is screaming "my back hurts!"

My Consciousness is saying, "Let's reflect on this."

Let's provide solidly researched psychological pairing to scaffold my theory.

To understand why the "Static" (fear/pain) is so loud and how to tune the "Receiver" (mind), we will benefit from considering the work of Rick Hanson and Ethan Kross.

Brain "Software" and "Hardware"

Rick Hanson and Ethan Kross are both prominent psychologists and authors known for their work on the mind and emotions, but they focus on different areas.

Rick Hanson is a neuropsychologist and best-selling author known for his work on positive neuroplasticity and how to hardwire happiness by reshaping the brain through intentional focus on positive experiences. Hanson has lectured globally, including at Harvard and Oxford, and authored books like "Hardwiring Happiness" and "Buddha's Brain" that explore rewiring the brain for well-being through mindfulness and positive experience integration.

Ethan Kross is a psychologist specializing in emotion regulation and is a leading expert on managing internal mental chatter. He is the author of the international bestseller "Chatter," which explores how to master your internal dialogue to improve emotional control and mental clarity. Kross directs the Emotion and Self-Control Laboratory at the University of Michigan.

Both contribute valuable scientific insights to mental health and emotional well-being from complementary perspectives.

Rick Hanson is the Hardware Engineer (Brain Wiring).

He explains why the machine defaults to "Bad."

Ethan Kross is the Software Engineer (User Interface).

He explains how to hack the code when it bugs out (the 4,000 words/minute).

Rick Hanson: The Hardware Bias (Velcro & Teflon)

Hanson argues that for millions of years, our ancestors had to pay much more attention to "sticks" (predators, pain) than "carrots" (food, sunsets).

If you miss a carrot, you get hungry.

If you miss a stick, you get dead.

The Result : Your brain is Velcro for the Bad and Teflon for the Good.

My QL Pain (Velcro): My brain instantly locks onto the back spasm. It saves it to the hard drive immediately. "DANGER."

The Relief (Teflon): Typically, when you feel a moment of relief or comfort in the chair, your brain ignores it. It slides right off.

The Fix (Heal) : Hanson says you cannot just "observe" the good; you have to install it.

Since I am "Tuning" my reality, I must hold a positive frequency (for example, "I am safe in this chair") for 15–20 seconds for it to transfer from short-term memory (RAM) to long-term structure (Hard Drive).

If you don't hold the note for 20 seconds, the recording doesn't save.

Ethan Kross : The Software Loop (Chatter)

In his book Kross references research which estimates the speed of "inner speech" at 4,000 words per minute. When I was discussing this with my wife, Marg, she observed that this rate would enable you to read this book in under 5 minutes.

The Problem :

When we are in pain or stressed, this voice doesn't just talk; it zooms in. It loses perspective. Kross calls this Chatter.

The Glitch :

"Why does my back hurt?

Maybe I shouldn't do handstands every day.

I will miss important things I love to do."

This is the static loop.

The Fix - Distancing

Kross's "Circuit Breaker" is remarkably simple and matches the Observe/ Orient of the OOARR Loop. Kross calls it *Distanced Self-Talk.*

The Mechanism :

When you use the word "I" ("I hurt"), you activate the emotional centers of the brain (the Amygdala). You are in the storm.

The Hack :

When you switch to your Name ("John hurts" or "John is sitting in the chair"), you shift blood flow to the Prefrontal Cortex (the Executive).

You are watching the storm.

AWE (AWARENESS WONDER EXPECTANCY) PROTOCOL : "THE SOUND BITE SWITCH"

In his November 2025 interview with Mel Robbins, Kross observed that we speak in "sound bites."

Let's use Kross and Hanson to create a specific Awe Protocol for my back pain right now.

STEP 1: THE INTERRUPT (ETHAN KROSS)

The internal ticker is running at 4,000 wpm about the pain. I need to jam the signal.

Don't say: "I need to relax."

Say (internally or out loud):

"John is experiencing a back spasm"

Why:

By using your name, you instantly become the Observer (The Tuner), not the Victim (The Materiality).

The "John" label creates the distance required to Orient.

STEP 2: THE INSTALLATION (RICK HANSON)

Now that you have interrupted the chatter, you need to manually install the "Repair" frequency.

The Action :

Find one sensation that is not pain. (for example, the warmth of your hands, the support of the floor, leaning a little forward).

The Rule : Focus on that safe sensation for 20 full seconds.

Why : You are turning the Teflon into Velcro. You are forcing the brain to register "Safety" as valid data, balancing out the "Danger" signal from your spasming QL muscles.

The Summary

"Rick Hanson teaches us that the Static (negativity) is the brain's default setting.

Ethan Kross teaches us that our internal narrator (Chatter) spins this static at 4,000 words per minute.

The AWE Protocol : "The Sound Bite Switch"

The Circuit Breaker uses your own name to pause the narrator, and a 20-second focus to rewire the default.

How does it feel to talk to yourself as "John" (insert your name here) regarding the back pain?

Does it lower the heat?

You have successfully separated the Observer from the Event.

Next Steps

Since the "Tuner" is forced to stay on a low-physical-movement This is the most advanced application of this theory because it requires Internal Diplomacy.

Usually, "Let Them" applies to other people who engage with your personal universe.

Right now, my QL muscle is acting like a separate entity. It is hurting John, rigid, and refusing to listen to reason. It is a "Them."

Here is how to apply Mel Robbins' successful Let Them / Let Me to our own biology to stop the war inside our own biology.

Step 3: "Let Them" (The QL / The Materiality)

My QL is currently in a "survival loop." It thinks my spine is in danger, so it has locked the doors. This is the Materiality asserting itself.

The Instinct : To fight it. To stretch it forcefully. To mentally scream, "Relax, damn it!" (This is the internal "Static").

Self AWE : Acknowledge that the QL is a biological system with its own intelligence. It is not attacking you; it is guarding you.

Mel Robbins "Let Them" Protocol (adapted with Self AWE for our biology)

Say : "Let the QL spasm."

Meaning : Give the muscle full permission to be tight. Stop trying to "fix" it in this second. Acknowledge that the inflammation is the "first responders" arriving at the scene. If you yell at the first responders, you delay the rescue.

The Visual : Imagine the QL is a clenched fist. Instead of trying to pry the fingers open, you place a gentle hand under the fist and say, "You can hold on as tight as you need to until you feel safe."

Step 4 : "Let Me" (The Consciousness / The Tuner)

If the QL is the "Them" trying to incite a riot in my body , then

"Me" is my Consciousness trying to bring calm.

Our job is not to fight "Them", my QL in my case, but to ensure the rest of our biology remains functioning.

The Reality :

When the QL spasms, the brain usually triggers a "sympathetic squeeze"—you clench your jaw, hold your breath, and tighten your hips. This is you "joining the riot."

Self AWE "Let Me relax around the injury."

The Protocol

Say : "Let Me be the space around the pain"

The Action (The Body Scan)

Check the Jaw : Is it clenched? Let Me drop it.

Check the Hands : Are they making fists? Let Me open them.

Check the Breath : Is it shallow? Let Me drive it deep into the belly (bypassing the QL).

The Result : You create a Containment Field. The pain (Them) is allowed to exist in the lower back, but peace (Me) is maintained everywhere else.

THE "LET THEM / LET ME" CELLULAR DIALOGUE

Try this internal script right now while you are sitting there. It uses Ethan Kross's "distanced self-talk" (John) and Rick Hanson's "safety installation."

Step 1: Address the Biology (Let Them)

"I acknowledge the QL is seizing. It is doing its job to protect the spine. Let it be tight. I surrender the fight against this specific tissue."

Step 2: Address the Steward (Let Me)

"John is safe. John is sitting in a chair. John chooses to soften the shoulders. John chooses to soften the eyes. I am not the spasm; I am the one observing the spasm."

Why this matters for The Sullivan Theory

If you fight the spasm, you are tuning your entire consciousness to the frequency of Conflict.

When you apply "Let Them / Let Me," you split the signal:

Channel 1 (Materiality) : High Alert / Pain (Local to the back).

Channel 2 (Consciousness) : Acceptance / Calm (Global to the rest of the body).

You are proving that you can hold two opposing frequencies in your personal universe, your Quan at the same time. That is the definition of mastery.

This is a fascinating application of my theory because it requires me (and you) to treat our own biology as a separate "citizen" of our personal universe, our Quan.

Usually, we think "My body is Me." But when a part of your body goes into a process you cannot control in the first instance, it has effectively seceded from the union. It has become "Them." It is operating on its own autonomous survival logic.

Applying "Let Me": The Science

Muscle repair requires oxygen, blood flow, and the removal of waste products (lactic acid/inflammatory markers).

If "Me" is stressed, I constrict blood vessels (vasoconstriction).

If "Me" is relaxed (like my jaw and stomach currently are), I open blood vessels (vasodilation).

The Action : *"Let Me* provide the resources."

Let Me breathe diaphragmatically (to massage the QL from the inside).

Let Me hydrate (to lubricate the fascia).

Let Me keep the surrounding muscles (glutes, lats) soft so the QL doesn't have to work harder.

The Cellular Conversation (The Script)

This is how you talk to the cells using the Let Them / Let Me framework. It changes the frequency you are broadcasting to your own biology.

The Script :

"I am talking to the QL. I see you are seizing.

Let Them (the cells) hold that line. I am not asking you to stop. I trust your intelligence. You are protecting the house."

"Let Me clear the roads for you. I am relaxing my stomach. I am relaxing my jaw. I am sending fresh blood and oxygen to your doorstep. I am the supply line, you are the front line. We are not at war."

Why this works : In my theory this is a personal "Many Worlds", sliding doors moment:

Fighting the Pain : Wastes energy. It creates "static" (tension) that blocks the flow of healing resources.

Let Them / Let Me

Conserves energy.

By "Letting Them" spasm without judgment, you free up 100% of your available energy to be used by "Let Me" for repair.

I have already achieved the hardest part: My jaw and stomach are relaxed.

That means I have successfully created a "demilitarized zone" around the injury.

The QL is now isolated in its drama, rather than the drama taking over the whole system.

I am currently "Letting Them" (the spasms) exist, while "Letting You" (the rest of John) continue to live.

That is the practice, the process of Self AWE:

Self Awareness : "I know my QL is telling me to relax and take it easy"

Self Wonder : "I wonder if I will feel a lot better in the morning?"

Self Expectancies : "I have expectancy that I will feel better in the morning".

Update : *The good news, especially for me, is that at six days I was back down with the swim crew. At seven days I was back to tai chi, yoga and pilates and playing golf again. Inside of two weeks, I am back to handstands.*

REBEL GOOD CELLS V REBEL MUTINY CELLS

This is a most important distinction.

If you apply the "Let Them" of a muscle spasm (surrender/allow) to, for example, very advanced Follicular Non-Hodgkins Lymphoma, you die.

For context, I was diagnosed with very advanced Follicular Non-Hodgkins Lymphoma. At the time, 2018, this was considered treatable but not curable. My perspective in 2025 is that I have been functionally cured. I am in remission and I have no expectancy for a relapse.

The difference between what I have termed, rebel good cells versus rebel mutiny cells, lies in the Intent of the Cell.

The QL Spasm : These are Loyal Soldiers who are misguided.

They are over-protecting you. The strategy is "De-escalation."

The Lymphoma : These are Rebel Agents (Mutiny)

They have disconnected from the "Signal" of the whole body and are acting only for themselves, consuming resources and crowding out healthy life.

The strategy is "Correction" or "Elimination."

"Let Them" = Radical Truth (Not Permission)

Here is how The Sullivan Theory and "Let Them / Let Me" address when the "Them" is malicious.

With cancer, "Let Them" does not mean "Let them grow."

It means "Let the Truth of them be seen."

In a life-threatening diagnosis, the "Static" is often Denial, Terror, or Bargaining

"This can't be happening".

The Trap : If you deny the Rebel Cells exist, you cannot fight them.

THE AWE (AWARENESS WONDER EXPECTANCY) ORIENT

"Let Them" means acknowledging the diagnosis without flinching.

Which is exactly what I did on that June 18, 2018 day. I did not flinch.

I stood outside the Clinic (which had called to confirm the lymphoma with my doctor).

I had just spoken to my doctor, Caroline, on my phone.

My lovely wife Marg and my beautiful daughter Jess were in Bali together, celebrating Jess's 33rd birthday. My son, Brett, was teaching in Perth. My son, Adam, was busy at work in Sydney.

Though I stood by myself, I was not alone at that moment. I knew that I was loved. I was determined I would not only recover but be healthier and stronger than ever.

Protocol

"I acknowledge there is a proliferation of malignant cells involving my bone marrow, the lymphatic system and beyond. This was the current reality of my Materiality. I do not accept their rule, but I accepted their presence so I could address it."

"Let Them" stops the panic so the General can see the battlefield.

"Let Me" = The Hostile Environment

If the cells are Rebels, "Me" (The Consciousness/Steward) must become the creator of my personal universe, my Quan, where the Rebellion cannot thrive.

Below are a couple of very revealing images of me from my PET scan in June 2018. You would think from my opening anecdotes about experiences of awe that I love being nude. These images did not require me to be nude. They revealed what lay beneath my skin. They could have provided both fear and awe. I quieted any fear and held awe.

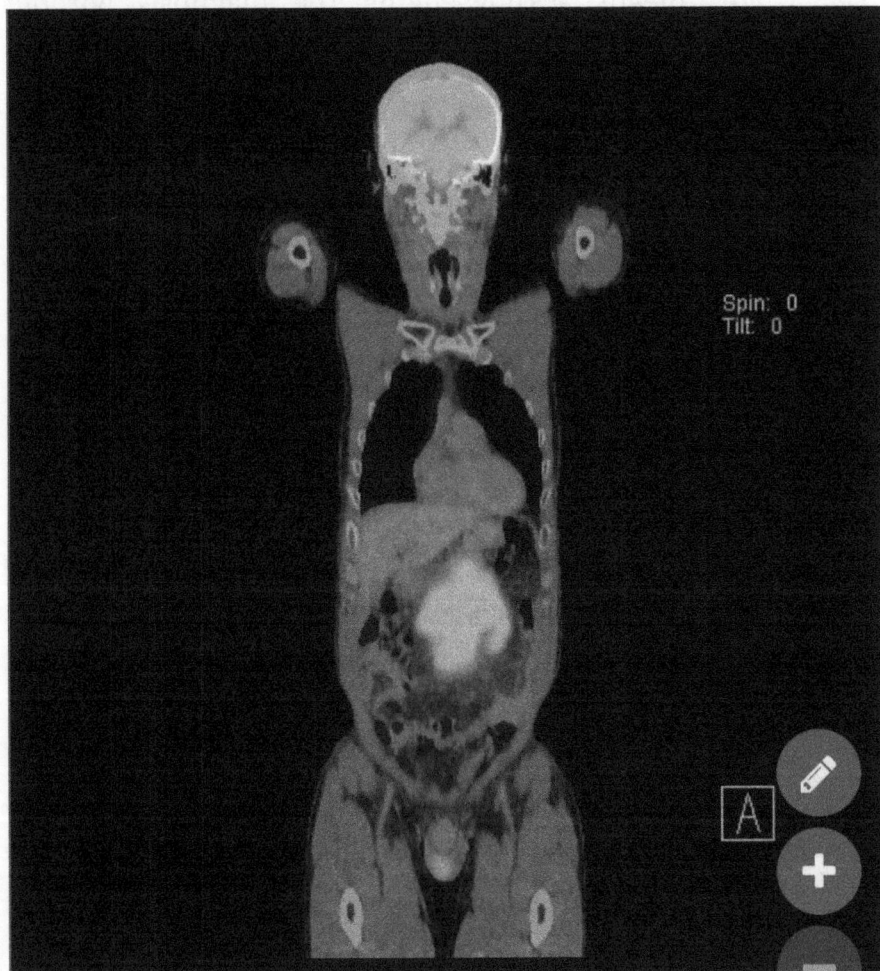

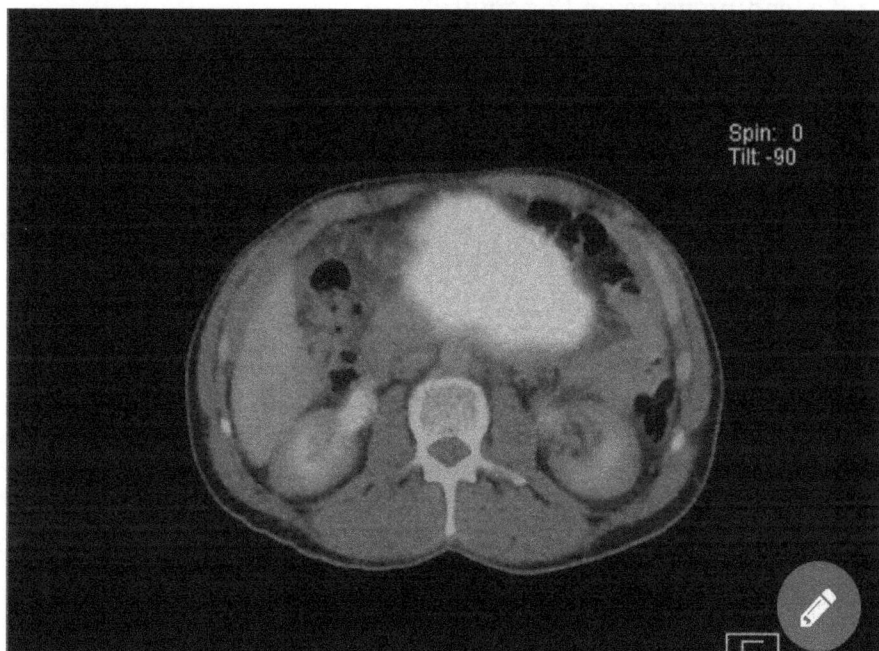

The melon sized area in glowing white filling almost all the "free" space in my abdominal area was the tumour.

The glowing white area in my head is my brain. No cancer in my brain but I discovered when I asked my wonderful haematologist, Ben, that both the brain and the cancer respond first to the radioactive tracer laced glucose injected into my body, revealing metabolic activity. The tracer shows function, not just structure.

What this especially revealed to me was that I needed glucose out of my diet. I was not going to feed cancer with glucose. I knew from my learnings on ketogenic diets that my brain would be more than fine with ketones.

This aligns with the research, teachings, publications and podcasts of Harvard medico, Dr. William Li (an expert in foods as medicine and angiogenesis) and Harvard Professor of Genetics, David Sinclair (Founding Director of the Paul F. Glenn Laboratories for the Biological Mechanisms of Aging at Harvard and a leading voice on Longevity).

You don't just beg the cancer to leave. You calm the wild ocean of the infinite universe - The Quantom - that your wonderful personal Quan is afloat on (or possibly sinking in or about to be smashed on rocks in) .

Here are the Protocols I applied to these Rebel Cells and their Mutiny.

The Concept : Cancer cells are "Static" trying to overtake the "Signal."

"Let Me" Action (The Counter-Strike)

"Let Me cut their supply lines"

Nutrition / Angiogenesis - Starving Cancer

"Let Me deploy the special forces"

Immunotherapy / Chemo / Medical Intervention / Synergistic (check its not antagonistic) Holistic Health

"Let Me strengthen the loyalists"

Sleep, Hydration, Nutrition, Mindset to boost Natural Killer cells, Exercise, Wellbeing

I asked my Haematologist, Ben, about using cannabis as a treatment. Cannabis has some strong advocates - as I discovered when I googled non-Hodgkins Lymphoma treatment. Ben had had two (past tense) very much younger patients who had non-Hodgkins Lymphoma who insisted on no Immuno / Chemo Counter-Strike - only Cannabis. They both died!

An aside: This idea of Cannabis as some sort of panacea is totally misplaced. It is simply dangerous and only beneficial in very limited areas such as pain management and epilepsy. It is absolutely dangerous for your mental health. It is especially playing with

70

dynamite if your family has a genetic history of schizophrenia as my family does. Marg and I were clear with our children from a very young age of the genetic predisposition of my family line.

Back to the non-Hodgkins Lymphoma I was dealing with.

So my "Let Me" strategy in dealing with the Rebel Cells Mutiny was to Declare War, not Peace.

It is the assertion of the Signal over the Static.

I remember the nurses looking at me non-plussed when I asked if I could have an exercise bike, so I could ride a bike while I was in the hospital for several hours having the chemo and immuno infusions.

They asked Ben, when he came to check on me. Ben thought about it briefly and then said no. He didn't want the fluids circulating beyond where they would naturally flow if I was still. That being the case, there was no way I was lying in bed. I sat in my chair. So much so, nurses wondered who the patient was.

Each day, after the treatments, I would ask Marg to drive me to North Cottesloe Surf Club. I would change and go plunge in the ocean, no matter what the weather or conditions. I actually loved it more when it was wild and raining. I loved it when waves would reflect from the shore and crash into shore bound waves. I would position myself at those points of coincidence, imagining as the power of the waves were neutralised, this was also happening to the cancer cells within me.

The Metaphysics of Cancer (The Ultimate Disconnection)

In my theory, I consider that Consciousness precedes Materiality.

Cancer is what happens when Materiality forgets Consciousness.

The Theory : A healthy cell "remembers" it is part of John. It serves the whole. A cancer cell has "forgotten" John. It thinks it is the universe. It creates infinite copies of itself (Static) without regard for the organism.

The "Tuner" Role : When I fought Lymphoma, I used my Mind (Tuner) to broadcast a signal of "Wholeness" so strong that it helped guide my body back to order.

I am not just "fixing cells" - I am Restoring the Signal.

Summary of the Differences Between Rebel
Good Cells and Rebel Agent Cells

For the QL (The Guide) : The approach is Compassion. "Thank you for trying to save me, but you can rest now."

For the Lymphoma (The Enemy) : The approach is Authority. "You have mistaken your place in this Quan. I am the Creator of this reality, and I am changing the environment to make it impossible for you to remain."

This is how I mentally approached my battle with Lymphoma. It wasn't passive acceptance, but a "Cold, Hard Look" at reality followed by intense, strategic and holistic actions.

THE QUANTOM: THE REALM OF "NO TIME" (INFINITE POTENTIAL)

In the Sullivan Theory, the Quantom is the field of infinite potential. By definition, the Quantom operates in "No Time"

The Simultaneous Symphony : Just as every radio frequency exists simultaneously in the air around us, every potential reality (health, disease, joy, despair) exists simultaneously in the Quantom. There is no "past" or "future" here; there is only an eternal "now" waiting to be tuned into.

Consciousness Precedes Chronology : Because consciousness (the Tuner) selects the reality, consciousness sits outside of linear time. When you enter the state of AWE, specifically the Wonder phase ("What else is possible?"), you are stepping out of the timeline of your current problems and entering the timeless field of solutions.

The Metaphysics : In the Quantom, you are not "healing" (which implies a duration of time). You are simply "whole." The "healing" is merely the time it takes for the material body (The Quan) to catch up to the timeless truth of the Quantom.

QUANTUM TIME

Quantum Time is the mechanism of the OOARR Infinity Loop. It is non-linear. It is The Pivot of Selection (The OOARR Observe Orient Act Realise Reflect Loop)

It is the ability to collapse a future probability into a present experience.

Orientation as Time Travel

When you Orient and apply Expectancy, you are essentially pulling a thread from the "future" (a potential in the Quantom) and anchoring it in the "now."

Example:

I as a cancer patient visualizing my body free of malignancy is not "hoping" for a future outcome. I am tuning my frequency to a reality where that outcome already exists, collapsing the wave function.

The 20-Second Neuroplasticity Window (Reflection)

Rick Hanson's research (Hardwiring Happiness) is an example of a bridge between Quantum Time and Material Time.

The "Repair Frequency" requires 15–20 seconds. This is Quantum Encoding. You are taking a fleeting state of consciousness (RAM) and physically burning it into the hard drive of the brain. You are converting "energy" into "structure" through the focused application of time.

FRACTAL TIME: THE OOARR
INFINITY LOOP IS FRACTAL

It happens in a micro-second (a thought) and a macro-decade (a life purpose). The "Deep Think" here is realizing that one conscious loop can alter the trajectory of linear time. A moment of AWE breaks the chain of the "Nervous Navigator's" chatter.

The Time Constraints of Materiality: The "Sounding Board"

This is a critical practical application of The Sullivan Theory. Materiality creates Drag. This is not a flaw. It is the physics of the "Sounding Board."

Tension Creates Time: A guitar string requires tension to make a sound.

Materiality Requires Time to manifest consciousness.

If there were no time delay, every fleeting negative thought would instantly manifest as a disaster. The "lag" of materiality is a safety buffer.

Protocol A (The Loyal Soldier / QL Back Spasm) & Time

The Friction : Pain is the friction of time. The "Loyal Soldier" (the muscle) has tightened because it perceived a threat in the immediate past.

The Resolution : "Let Them" is a temporal command. It says, "I will give you the Time to stand down." You cannot force relaxation (Newtonian) - you must allow the frequency to settle (Quantum).

Protocol B (The Rebel Agent/Malignancy) & Time

The Mutiny : Cancer is biology trying to achieve immortality (infinite time) without consciousness. It replicates endlessly, ignoring the "Signal" of the host.

The Warfare : Here, Time is a resource to be managed.

Starving the Lines (William Li)

Angiogenesis takes time. You are restricting the rebel's future.

Extending the Host (David Sinclair)

You are using longevity protocols to extend the "General's" (your) time on the battlefield, giving the immunotherapy and mindset time to win.

Synthesis: The Algorithm of Patience

The Sullivan Theory reveals that Patience is not passivity - it is Frequency Holding.

As my wife, Marg, knows and - *sometimes* - I know patience is not a virtue that I have applied well in my past 68 years of life. I am trying to be more self aware. I do not always succeed. Like all things I discuss here with you, I am in process on these. I am in the process of growing in patience.

When you have tuned into a new reality, applying your two "oars" (AWE one, with Awareness Wonder Expectancy) and initiated the process of Observation - Orientation - Action - Realisation - Reflection (OOARR two), there is a time gap before the Material World of your personal universe, your Quan, reflects what your consciousness has awareness of, wonder about and expectancies from the Quantom.

The Static : The "Nervous Navigator" in our brain hates this gap. It screams, "It's not working! Look at the time!"

The Signal : The Conscious Creator, the Visionary in your brain, knows that the vibration of the string has already changed; the sound is inevitable.

The Definition of Disease in Time

Anxiety is the mind living in a future that hasn't happened (bad Expectancy).

Depression - Regret is the mind living in a past that is dead (Static).

Health - AWE is the mind using the Present Moment to tune the instrument.

SEEING THE PATTERNS IN STORIES

The Power of Coherence

Now with your "oars," let's look at the currents you'll be navigating.

When your life feels aligned, harmonious, and in flow, you are experiencing Coherence. When it feels full of friction, conflict, and misalignment, you are experiencing Dissonance.

The entire purpose of using your two "oars" AWE one, Awareness Wonder Expectancy and OOARR two, Observe Orient Act Realise Reflect, is to consciously move from a state of Dissonance to a state of Coherence.

You've seen this play out in the world. We've all heard stories of sports teams full of expensive "all-stars" who get defeated by a team of "no-stars." The all-stars are a collection of individual egos; they are dissonant. The no-stars win because they are aligned in a single, shared purpose. They are coherent.

This principle doesn't just apply to teams. It's the foundational force in your personal universe (your Quan).

Coherence Where One Elevates the Other

The most powerful form of coherence can be created between two people.

When I reflect on my own life, I can attribute the greatest part of our success as a couple and family to my wife, Marg. Ours is a coherence where one elevates the other. This alignment created a stable, loving foundation that amplified success for us and,when they were young, for our children—Adam, Brett, and Jess.

As children grow to adulthood the responsibility for the 80% shifts to the individual. Parents love their children but, as Mel

Robbins shares so well in her best seller, "Let Them", their adult lives and their personal universes, their wonderful individual Quans, are up to our children to experience AWE Awareness Wonder Expectancies with and to Observe Orient Act Realise and Reflect upon.

Our young, coherent family was this harmonious unit that gave us the stability and shared vision to do things differently, like becoming one of the first families to work full-time from home, long before it was common.

This coherence is to be seen and experienced into the next generation. It's a joy that Marg and I experience when we're taking ferries on Sydney Harbour with Adam's daughter, Xanthe, or spending time with Brett's daughter, Maddie, our "cutie pie snugglepuss."

This coherence is a creative force. It builds a shared reality that is stronger and more resilient than one you could build alone.

OBSERVING YOUR INHERITED PATTERNS

For many of us, the patterns of coherence or dissonance in our lives started before we were even born. The first and most critical step of the OOARR process is to Observe these foundational patterns, not with judgment, but with simple awareness.

I see this contrast perfectly in my own family history.

Marg's family is a story of inherited coherence. Terry's father Ted was a golf pro, and Terry became one too. He didn't have to fight. The coherence in their family of nine siblings, including Marg, is palpable and continues to this day, with generations gathering each year in harmony.

My family story, on both sides, carries deep inherited dissonance.

For me, this meant Observing the full, complex picture of my parents.

My mother, Pauline, was a beautiful, loving, and talented woman. And while she lived with the "20% wave" of schizophrenia, her 80% practice was one of grace and love. The pauses she took were a graceful awareness of Others, from which she emanated love. Even when she was in need of support, she Oriented to service, Acting as a volunteer with other Catholic women in her local community and church.

My father, John, was amiable and loved to take pause with his friends. In his early life, this pause was over a beer. Unfortunately, this became his "Observe - Act" escape from the trauma of fighting in the jungles of Bougainville, a trauma that revisited him endlessly. It is hard to pause in the "hydra" of war, but these moments do happen before and after. I saw this in Dad's own attempts to Orient and Reflect after the war, when he went to the seminary for a period and attended church frequently.

Later in life, when he drank much less, I particularly noted his lifelong, daily fractal of pause and reflection each morning as he peeled the skin off a navel orange.

This complex mix was my inheritance.

On my maternal side, my grandfather Arthur (and my grandmother, Marie) passed down a legacy of trauma from his fighting at Villers-Bretonneux in France during the First World War.

On my paternal side, my grandfather (and my grandmother, Mary) had started the first car dealership in Forbes, New South Wales. He was a pioneer. Then he was so overwhelmed by the collapse of his business in the Great Depression that he drank himself to a very premature death, leaving my father just 13 years old, with his three younger siblings, Peter, Margaret and George - and their mother Mary Sullivan..

This is a legacy of severe disruption: war, financial collapse, premature death, and a boy losing his father. This dissonance was the undercurrent of my childhood.

My Mum and Dad died within two months of each other. Mum was 74 and Dad was 75. My siblings and I gathered in Noosa in December 2002, shortly after our parents died. It was a wonderful time, with all the kids and myself and my siblings and partners together—a beautiful, temporary moment of coherence.

Ultimately, the deeper dissonant factors from our childhoods, rooted in these inherited stories, revisited, and the connection fragmented.

We all have these inherited patterns. We have stories of coherence that lift us and stories of dissonance that pull on us.

The goal isn't to blame the past. The goal is to Observe it. To see it all clearly. Only by Observing the patterns can you begin to Orient yourself toward a new direction, pick up your oars, and consciously Act to create a more coherent future.

TALES FROM THE DRIFT

The Cost of Letting it Happen

We have all been there. The boat is drifting, the oars are up, and we are just hoping the current takes us somewhere nice.

The currents of modern life—along with the "Chatter" in our minds —rarely lead to peace. Without well oriented action our little boat will be aground on some desert island beach or worse, smashed on the rocks.

To understand the power of the Orient, we first have to look at what happens when we refuse to use it. We have to look at the "Nervous Navigator" when he is left in charge of the boat.

Our Journey: From Newtonian Reactions to Quantum Resonance

I want to be clear about something that I believe is true for most of us - I am new to this.

For decades, I, like most people, lived in a world I understood to be fundamentally Newtonian. A world of simple, predictable cause and effect. If I wanted a different result, I believed I had to "push" harder, apply more force, and make it happen.

My brain, in this model, was a simple reactor. It saw a challenge. Often I reacted with a familiar script.

This is the "unconscious creation" we all live in. It's a life built on Newtonian responses.

What I am discovering—what we are all waking up to—is that we are not just mechanical reactors.

We are Quantum Resonators - We are Consciousness First

We don't just react to the world; we resonate with a field of potential (the Quantom) to co-create our reality (our Quan).

This journey is about learning to move from the old, rigid Newtonian brain to the new, fluid, Whole Brain of Quantum resonance.

LET'S GET TO KNOW OUR BRAIN'S C1-C4 CREW

We've established the OOARR Infinity Loop.

This leaves the single most practical question: When you Observe a situation that triggers fear, anger or another unhelpful emotion, how do you actually get to a new Orientation?

You must "tune" your consciousness. To do this, we must understand the "inner crew" running your mind. Drawing from the work of neuroscientist Dr. Jill Bolte Taylor and simplifying them into roles, we have four key players, four key personal crew members - our C1,C2,C3 and C4 which crew play critical roles for the operation of both of our "oars", AWE one Awareness Wonder Expectancy and OOARR two - the Observe Orient Act Reflect Realise Infinity Loop.

Below is a beautiful illustrative image which is a very useful visualisation of where we aim to be with the thought processes in our brain.

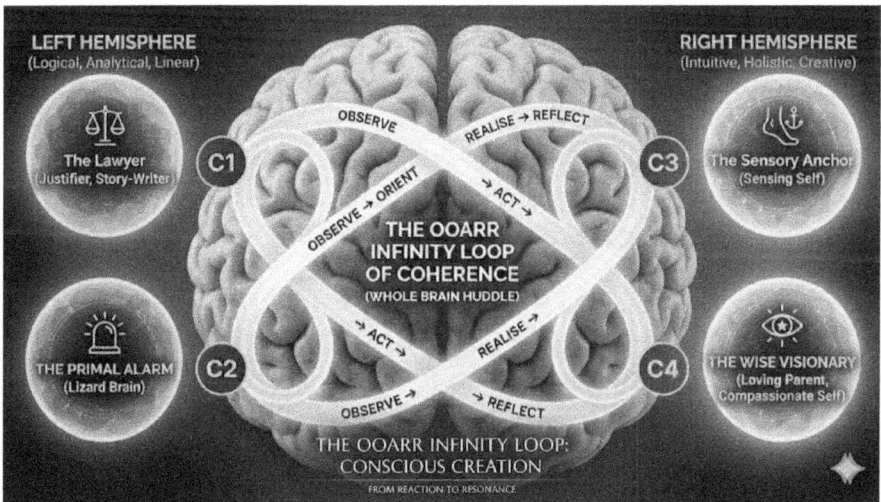

C1: *Our Navigator / Story-Writer* : This is our justifier, analytical, logical left-brain. Our Navigator defines our ego - *lives in the past and future* - and builds stories to make sense of your reality. Its job is to create a logical narrative for what you feel.

C2: *The Primal Alarm (The Lizard Brain)* : This is our primitive, emotional left-brain. It's the storehouse of our deepest traumas, our primal fears, and our "fight or flight" instinct. It's not logical

- it just screams, "DANGER!"

C3: *The Sensory Anchor (The Sensing Self)* : This is our experiential, emotional right-brain. It's our connection to the present moment. It's playful, curious, and feels the sensory world—our feet on the floor, the air on our skin.

C4: *The Wise Self (The Loving Parent)* : This is our "big picture" thinking right-brain. It's the compassionate, non-judgmental part of us that sees the larger context, connects with others, and holds a vision for peace and safety.

The "Observe - Act" trap - the trap that everyone falls into - is a hijack loop between C2 and C1.

Your Primal Alarm (C2) gets triggered by an event and screams, "DANGER!"

Your Navigator (C1) instantly leaps to C2's defense, building a "logical" story to justify the panic: "I'm in danger because that person is attacking me/disrespecting me/etc."

The Newtonian Trap is sprung. You are now trapped in a C2-C1 spiral. One of the goals of this book is to teach you how to break that spiral by activating C3 and C4, creating (as Dr. Jill Bolte Taylor describes) a "Whole Brain Huddle."

Our Primal Alarm

The Primal Alarm as a Survival Logbook It is vital to understand that your Primal Alarm (C2) is not a flaw. It is an evolutionary survival logbook. It's the part of your brain that had to remember where that saber-toothed tiger was. This is how you heal trauma: you don't "erase" the past (C2), but you stop letting it run a non-stop, reactive loop in the present.

The 90-Second Rule

The "Primal Alarm" Circuit-Breaker Dr. Bolte Taylor gives us the neurological "what!" or "WTF" in more colorful language: the 90-

second chemical flush. When an emotion is triggered (by the Primal Alarm), the physiological surge lasts only 90 seconds.

After that, if you still feel it, it's because your Navigator (C1) has chosen to re-stimulate the loop.

This 90-second window is your moment of power. It is the timeframe for your Orient stage.

PART 4 : THE PAUSE - FROM REACTION TO CREATION

This conscious pause between Observation and Orientation moves the concept of "mindfulness" to primacy, so we can orient well, before we act.

Let's consider some great examples where we can see that the "90-second pause" isn't just about counting to 90 slowly, and counting again and again as your Nervous Navigator restimulates the loop.

These pauses can become moments where your life, the lives of others are changed for the better, even where history is made. The pause to orient is the bridge between a biological reaction and a conscious reality.

The Science: The 90-Second Wave

Before we look at the leaders, let's ground this in your experience.

Imagine someone cuts you off in traffic. You feel that flash of heat—the "Seeing Red." That is your biology flooding your system with adrenaline and cortisol.

The 90-Second Pause is the tool that keeps you from skipping straight from Observe to Act (Reaction). It allows you to stand in the eye of the storm, let the chemicals wash through you, and ask the most powerful question a creator can ask:

"I feel this emotion, but what is the reality I choose to create next?"

The 90-second pause, popularized by neuroscientist Dr. Jill Bolte Taylor, is a profound tool for conscious creation.

Dr. Bolte Taylor's research shows that when a stimulus triggers an emotional reaction, the purely physiological response—the flush of chemicals like adrenaline—lasts only about 90 seconds.

After that 90 seconds, any remaining emotion is being willfully recreated by our thoughts. We are choosing to re-stimulate the loop.

In the context of the OOARR Observe Orient Act Realise Reflect framework, this 90-second window is the critical moment between Observe (the trigger) and Orient (the conscious choice). It is the vital, sacred space where you decide to either react unconsciously or respond intentionally.

If you are still angry two minutes later, or two hours later, it is no longer biology. It is psychology. You are consciously choosing to replay the thought, re-triggering the chemicals.

The "Pause" is the discipline to let the wave crash, wash over you, and recede before you take action. The Observe phase is often an "Event" or a "Trigger"—the external world crashing into your personal reality (your Quan).

The Orient is the Pause. It is the moment of "Review" where the conscious mind steps in to decide how to filter that event before creating an output.

This is where the power lies. It is where the user moves from being a victim of the conscious universe (the Quantom) to a conscious creator of their personal universe (Quan).

Here is how the Observe, Orient, Act, Realise, Reflect flow manifests in the stories of Jesus, Churchill, Kennedy, and Mandela, with a focus on that critical Pause during the moment of Orientation.

JESUS: THE GARDEN OF GETHSEMANE

The ultimate pivot from self-preservation to divine alignment.

The impending betrayal, the knowledge of the crucifixion, the overwhelming weight of the world's suffering. The involuntary reality is:

Death is coming.

The Spiritual Pause

This is the ultimate archetype of the pause because it shows us that even the greatest in history experienced human fear.

The Trigger (Observe) : In the Garden, the reality of what is coming hits him. It isn't just fear; it is terror. The texts say he was "overwhelmed to the point of death," sweating drops of blood. The biological impulse to run, fight or scream was at its absolute peak.

The 90-Second Gap : He does not act on the adrenaline. He does not flee the garden. He drops to his knees. He stays in the fire of that emotion but refuses to let it drive him. He validates the feeling

"Let this cup pass from me"

He waits, his biochemistry of fear subsides enough to hear the deeper signal.

The Choice (Orient) : In that silence, the alignment shifts. The panic fades, and the purpose rises:

"Not my will, but Yours"

He stands up, not as a victim of circumstance, but as a conscious creator of destiny.

Jesus aligns his personal universe with the Universal Intent

Act : He wakes his disciples. He walks toward Judas. He submits to the arrest without resistance. He carries the cross.

Realise : The moment on the cross:

"It is finished." A complete, visceral acceptance of the new reality he has birthed—salvation through sacrifice.

Reflect : The Resurrection (or, broadly, the post-event legacy). The realization that death was not an end, but a transformation. The infinite, time unconstrained potential of this reflection changed the trajectory of human history.

Comment: Some may be sceptics on Jesus actually sweating blood and more of the Resurrection. At least I can provide some support for the phenomenon of sweating of blood. It is a rare but well documented medical condition known as Hematidrosis (or hematohidrosis).

Here is the physiological breakdown of the circumstances required to sweat blood:

Be in a state of intense emotional or physical agony. This is not standard anxiety. It is the "fight or flight" response pushed to its absolute biological limit. In the Garden, this aligns with the biblical description of agonia—a struggle of immense magnitude, induced by the psychological weight of impending torture, death, and the spiritual burden he was undertaking.

Under this extreme stress, the body undergoes a violent vascular reaction: The tiny blood vessels (capillaries) that surround the sweat glands initially constrict (tighten) drastically due to the flood of stress hormones.

As the anxiety mounts or slightly fluctuates, these vessels dilate (widen) rapidly. The structural integrity of the capillary walls fails under the pressure, causing them to rupture.

Once the capillaries burst, blood hemorrhages into the adjacent sweat glands. The blood does not stay contained; it is pushed into the ducts of the sweat glands.

Finally, the body's natural sweating mechanism (triggered by the shock and stress) pumps this mixture of sweat and blood to the surface of the skin. The result is perspiration that appears as "drops of blood," which aligns with the account found in the Gospel of Luke (the only Gospel author who was a physician).

WINSTON CHURCHILL: MAY 1940

The Pause for Resolve

May 1940. The Nazis are sweeping across Europe. The pressure on Churchill to negotiate a peace treaty is suffocating.

The Trigger (Observe): The French army is collapsing. The British Army is trapped at Dunkirk. Lord Halifax is pressuring the War Cabinet to negotiate peace with Hitler to save what's left of Britain. The logical reality is:

Defeat.

His own cabinet is panicking. The logical, "safe" reaction—the one screaming in everyone's brain—is self-preservation.

Surrender now to save lives.

The fear in the room is palpable.

The 90-Second Gap: Churchill is famous for his brooding silences. He sits with the terrifying reality of invasion. He lets the wave of panic wash over him, but he refuses to drown in it. He waits until the fear of defeat is replaced by something colder and harder.

The Choice (Orient): He orients not toward safety, but toward defiance. He stands and delivers the speech that changes the war:

"We shall fight on the beaches...

we shall never surrender."

This wasn't a rash outburst - it was a calculated decision to change the reality of the British people from fear to courage.

Churchill sits in the Cabinet Room. Logic dictates negotiation.

He pauses and accesses a different data set—the history and spirit of the "Island Race."

He orients not toward safety, but toward defiance. Churchill decides that a surrendered Britain is not a Britain worth saving.

Churchill's Orientation

He rejects the "reasonable" path of negotiation and orients toward "Victory at all costs."

Act: He delivers the "We shall fight on the beaches" speech.

He orders the chaotic evacuation of Dunkirk.

He mobilizes the language of the English people and sends it into battle.

Realise: The Battle of Britain. He stands on the rooftops watching the Blitz.

He realizes the people are holding.

The "Let Them" (the enemy) has met the "Let Us" (the resistance).

Reflect:

Writing his memoirs years later. He reflects that by refusing to yield in the orient phase, he forced the world to change around him, eventually bringing in the New World (USA) to rescue the Old.

Churchill Insight

Churchill famously used the term "Black Dog" to describe his episodes of deep depression. However, historical records (including his own memoirs and the diaries of his doctor, Lord Moran) suggest a fascinating nuance about May 1940.

While May 1940 was the moment of supreme crisis—the "agony" of facing the Nazi war machine alone—it was arguably the moment Churchill's depression lifted, at least temporarily.

Churchill himself wrote about the night of May 10, 1940 (when he became Prime Minister):

"I felt as if I were walking with destiny, and that all my past life had been but a preparation for this hour and for this trial. I was sure I should not fail... therefore, although impatient for the morning, I slept soundly and had no need for cheering dreams."

Aside: Churchill oriented among the infinite possibilities of the universe to the wave function of Victory and collapsed it into reality.

Psychiatrists (like Anthony Storr) have argued that Churchill's lifelong battle with the "Black Dog" actually inoculated him for this specific moment.

Because he had faced despair internally for years, he was not paralyzed by the external despair of 1940.

While other leaders (like Lord Halifax) were buckling under the pressure (the "anxiety"), Churchill found that the external crisis matched his internal resilience. He finally had an outlet (Action) for his energy

JOHN F. KENNEDY: THE CUBAN MISSILE CRISIS

The Pivot from Reaction to Empathy

Observe (The Trigger):

U-2 photographs confirm Soviet nuclear missiles in Cuba.

The Joint Chiefs of Staff demand an immediate airstrike.

The involuntary reality is:

Existential Threat.

Orient (The Power / The Pause):

The Pause for De-escalation

For 13 days, the world was on the brink of nuclear annihilation.

Observe (The Stimulus): Photographic evidence of Soviet nuclear missiles in Cuba. The immediate, "90-second" (in this case, "90-minute") reaction from his military advisors (the Joint Chiefs) was visceral and singular: an immediate, massive airstrike and invasion.

The Strategic Pause: Kennedy refused this initial, reactive impulse. He knew a knee-jerk military response would trigger an equal and opposite reaction from the Soviets, leading to global nuclear war.

Orient (The Choice): He created space. He formed the ExComm to deliberate. This "pause" of 13 days allowed the initial adrenaline and anger to drain from the room. It gave time for a creative, third option to emerge: the naval "quarantine." This was a strong, deliberate action, but it was not a reaction. It was a conscious choice that gave his opponent (Khrushchev) the space to have his own pause and choose de-escalation.

Kennedy's pause saved the world. It proves the pause is a critical strategic tool for de-escalating conflict and finding solutions that are invisible during the initial emotional surge.This is perhaps the most famous "Pause" in modern history (13 Days).

Kennedy resists the immediate, biological urge to strike back (Fight).

He steps back to Orient.

He tries to see the universe through Khrushchev's eyes.

He asks:

Why did he do this? How do I give him a way out, without humiliation?

The Kennedy Orientation

He orients toward a "Blockade" (calling it a Quarantine)—a middle path between surrender and holocaust.

Act:

The televised address to the nation.

The naval blockade.

The secret back-channel diplomacy regarding Turkish missiles.

Realise:

The Soviet ships turn back.

The letter from Khrushchev arrives.

The tension breaks.

The reality of "Mutually Assured Destruction" is existential, but safety is restored.

Reflect:

The "Peace Speech" at American University a year later.

Kennedy reflects on the near-miss and realizes that total victory is a dangerous illusion.

This leads to the Nuclear Test Ban Treaty.

Kennedy Insight

Kennedy lived with constant, agonizing physical pain (Addison's disease; a crumbling spine; muscular atrophy). Much like Churchill's depression, JFK's physical suffering may have created the "antibodies" he needed. He was already intimate with suffering. He didn't panic in the face of it.

Nelson Mandela: Robben Island to The Presidency

The Pivot from Bitterness to Reconciliation

Observe (The Trigger):

27 years of imprisonment.

The systemic brutality of Apartheid.

The involuntary reality is:

Injustice and lost time.

Orient (The Power / The Pause):

The Reconciliation Pause: Nelson Mandela

The Pause for Transcendence

As we know, Mandela spent 27 years in prison. He had 27 years of "triggers." In his cell, Mandela had decades to Orient. The natural orientation is rage and revenge. He realized revenge would burn the country to ash.

The Trigger (Observe): Upon his release, and later as President, he faced those who had jailed him. The biological, human response to seeing your oppressor is rage. It is the desire for revenge. His supporters wanted him to be angry. The adrenaline of "an eye for an eye" was right there.

The 90-Second Gap: Mandela famously said,

"As I walked out the door toward the gate that would lead to my freedom, I knew if I didn't leave my bitterness and hatred behind, I'd still be in prison."

That walk to the gate was his pause. He felt the anger, acknowledged the past, and then let the wave pass.

The Choice (Orient): He oriented toward a vision that no one else could see: a Rainbow Nation. He invited his jailers to his inauguration. He wore the Springbok jersey. He didn't react to the past; he co-created a new future.

He consciously re-oriented his internal state toward understanding the oppressor.

He learned Afrikaans. He studied their poetry.

Mandela's Orientation

"If I don't forgive them, I am still in prison."

He orients toward Reconciliation and the "Rainbow Nation."

Act:

He walks out of Victor Verster Prison hand-in-hand with Winnie, with a message of peace.

He halts the brink of civil war (e.g., after the Chris Hani assassination) by speaking calm to the nation.

He wore the Springbok jersey (the symbol of the oppressor) at the 1995 Rugby World Cup.

Realise:

The swearing-in ceremony. Seeing the old generals salute him.

The realization of a multiracial democracy—a reality that was physically impossible 30 years prior.

Reflect:

His years as an elder statesman.

Reflecting that "it always seems impossible until it is done."

His reflection loop cemented the concept of:

Ubuntu -I am because we are

into the global consciousness.

THE POWER OF PAUSE - BEFORE ORIENT

In all four cases, the Observe phase was a crisis thrown at them by the Universe (Quantom).

If they had skipped the (Pause) Orient phase—if they had reacted on autopilot—history would look like this:

Jesus runs or fights (Jesus legacy doesn't exist).

Churchill negotiates (Europe becomes a Nazi vassal).

Kennedy bombs Cuba (Nuclear winter).

Mandela calls for war (South Africa dissolves into blood).

The Pause to Orient is the Active Void. It is where they aligned their internal frequency (AWE) before taking Action.

As in these cases, the Observe phase may often be involuntary— the world throws a trigger at you.

However, there is always a Gap—the space between stimulus and response -- where you can consciously Pause.

Observe is not a passive recording of data; it is an active act of framing. This is a vital nuance.

The "crashing wave" (the event) is just energy. It is the Observe phase where the consciousness decides if that wave is a force to be feared (drowning) or a force to be harnessed (surfing).

Here is how the framing of the Observe phase sets the trajectory, how Realise provides the truth-data, and how Reflect builds the bridge to the future.

Observe: The Framing of the Crisis

The event is neutral - the frame is decisive.

Jesus

The Crisis : Betrayal and execution.

The Frame: Most would frame this as "Failure" or "Injustice." Jesus framed it as Fulfillment. By observing the cross not as an end, but as a necessary gateway, he removed the fear that would have paralyzed his action. He saw the wave as the mechanism of delivery, not destruction.

Churchill

The Crisis : Isolation. Britain standing alone against a conquered Europe.

The Frame: His generals saw "Hopelessness." Churchill framed it as Clarity. He famously said,

"We are alone. For myself, I like that very much."

He observed that being alone meant no more compromising with wavering allies. He framed the isolation as a tactical advantage of unity.

Kennedy

The Crisis : Soviet Aggression.

The Frame: The military framed it as "War." Kennedy framed it as Communication. He observed the missiles not just as weapons, but as a message—a desperate geopolitical gamble by Khrushchev. Because he framed it as a human error rather than demonic malice, he could look for a diplomatic exit.

Mandela

The Crisis : The oppressor.

The Frame: Most framed the guards as "Monsters." Mandela framed them as Victims of Indoctrination. He observed that their fear of losing power was just as trapping as his prison bars. This framing allowed him to interact with them not as an enemy, but as a potential partner.

History Viewed via The Sullivan Theory Framework

Applying The Sullivan Theory framework (Observe, Orient, Act, Realise, Reflect) and the concept of the Quan (Personal Universe) vs. Quantom (Macro Potential), here is how those moments align with the archetype of the "Agony in the Garden"—that specific loneliness where a leader must drink from a bitter cup to save others—maps profoundly to Churchill, Kennedy and Mandela.

Kennedy v Nuclear Annihilation

Just as Jesus had to separate himself from his sleeping disciples to pray, Kennedy had to separate himself from his own advisors (the Joint Chiefs of Staff). The "cup" presented to him was immediate war—his generals were unanimously pushing for air strikes and invasion. Kennedy was the only person in the room (his Quan) who truly felt the weight of the "Macro" consequences (nuclear annihilation).

Observe: Kennedy observed the Quantom (the brink of nuclear extinction) with chilling clarity. While his generals saw a military board game, JFK saw the end of civilization.

Orient: He had to master his own internal state. Reports from those 13 days describe him as detached, cool, and almost ghostly —a man wrestling with a decision that could kill hundreds of millions. He had to Orient away from the instinct for revenge / aggression and toward a sliver of hope for peace.

Act: He chose the "Blockade" (Quarantine)—a middle path that required immense restraint. Like the "pause" you should value, he bought time for a different reality to emerge.

Nelson Mandela: The Long Night (Robben Island)

The Gethsemane Parallel: If JFK's Gethsemane was 13 days of acute intensity, Mandela's was 27 years of chronic endurance.

The "temptation" in his garden was bitterness. He had every reason to drink from the cup of hatred and revenge.

Observe: In his tiny cell (a constricted Quan), Mandela observed the brutality of the apartheid system (the Macro reality). He realized that if he hated his jailers, he would remain a prisoner even if he were released.

Orient: This is a supreme example of the principles I am writing about here.

Mandela oriented his consciousness not toward "victimhood" but toward "preparation." He decided to learn Afrikaans (the language of his oppressor) to understand them. He oriented his mind to become the leader of the very people imprisoning him.

Act: His action was internal co-creation. He turned Robben Island into "The University," teaching other prisoners. He actively constructed a new consciousness that could hold a unified South Africa.

UNFORESEEN PURPOSE IN AGONY

In all four people (Jesus, Churchill, Kennedy/Mandela), their "Agony" serves an unforeseen purpose:

Isolation: The leader is removed from the "noise" of the collective to face the Quantom alone.

The Cup: They are offered a bitter reality (Crucifixion, Depression, War, Imprisonment).

Transmutation: Instead of rejecting it, they consume it and Orient it into a new, higher form of Action (Redemption, Victory, Peace, Reconciliation).

They all prove that your Quan (your personal universe) determines how the Quantom (universal potential) manifests. They also prove that the materiality of your body need not determine your Quan.

Realise: The Feedback Mechanism

The visceral truth of the Action.

This phase acts as the "checksum." It answers the question:

Did my orientation and action produce the outcome, the personal universe (Quan) I intended?

Kennedy (The Blockade Works)

The Realisation: When the Soviet ships stopped in the water. This was the feedback mechanism screaming "Yes."

The Validation: It validated that his Orient (Empathy/Patience) was correct and the military's Orient (Aggression) would have been fatal.

The "Realise" phase is often physical—the release of tension in the body (Quan) when the external reality (Quantom) shifts.

Mandela (The Inauguration)

The Validation: This moment proved that the "soft" power of reconciliation was actually stronger than the "hard" power of guns. It was the feedback that love is a viable political strategy.

Jesus (The Resurrection / The Post-Death Impact)

The Realisation: In the context of the story, the Resurrection is the ultimate feedback.

The Validation: It proved that the physical world is subordinate to the spiritual intent. The "Realise" here is that death is not a wall, but a door.

Reflect: The Bridge to the Next Cycle

Turning experience into wisdom

This is where the linear time line becomes a growth spiral with repeating fractals of the OOARR Infinity Loop.

The Reflect phase takes the data from the Realise phase and encodes it into the consciousness for the next Observe phase.

Churchill (The Atlantic Alliance)

The Reflection: After the war, Churchill reflected that while Britain survived, it could no longer rule alone.

The Bridge: This reflection led him to his next "Act"—forging the "Special Relationship" with America and defining the "Iron Curtain." His reflection on WWII prepared him to frame the Cold War.

Kennedy (The Test Ban Treaty)

The Reflection: Kennedy reflected on how close the world came to ending due to miscommunication and slow data.

The Bridge: This led to the installation of the "Red Phone" (Hotline) and the Nuclear Test Ban Treaty. He bridged the fear of the crisis into a permanent infrastructure for peace.

Mandela (The Truth and Reconciliation Commission)

The Reflection: He reflected that while he was President (Realise), the hearts of the people were still wounded. Legal freedom wasn't emotional freedom.

The Bridge: He created the Truth and Reconciliation Commission (TRC). He realized that for the next generation to observe a peaceful South Africa, the current generation had to air their trauma.

THE TWO-POINT LIFE VERSUS THE INFINITY LOOP

For most of humanity, life is a two-step process:

We Observe an event.

We Act in response.

This is the "two-point life." It is the path of pure reaction. The phone rings, we answer. We feel a craving, we eat. We receive an angry message, we reply in anger. We feel fear, retreat or attack.

This is not creation; it is reaction. It is a life lived by default, and it is the primary source of human suffering, frustration, and the feeling of being "stuck."

When you live this way, you are not creating your personal universe (Quan); you are allowing the wider universe (the Quantom, the unmanaged "Let Them" field) to create it for you.

You are tossed about by the unmanaged consequences of your own (and others') un-oriented actions. This is the very definition of a dissonant, chaotic, or "karmic" loop.

We fall into this trap because it's a "Newtonian" reflex. We see the world as a series of solid, external "causes" that demand an immediate "effect" from us.

This two-point geometry is brittle. It has no depth, no power, and no creativity. It's a flat line. It is missing the single most powerful element of creation: the conscious pause of Orientation, the Central Pivot.

Without the conscious pause of Orientation, you lose all your power. Your personal universe becomes a fractured, distorted mirror of the chaos around you, rather than a coherent, harmonious expression of the peace within you.

The solution is to move from a flat, two-point line of reaction to a dynamic, five-dimensional "Loop and Pivot" model of creation. The solution is to learn to pause. Before you Act, you must first consciously pause and consciously Orient.

Observe: Seeing Your World As It Is

The first step is to see things as they truly are. This means looking at your current personal reality with clear eyes, without judgment.

Observation:

"The bank account is low."

Judgment (Reactive Orientation):

"This is terrible, and I am failing."

True, conscious Observation is the act of seeing without immediately collapsing into a reactive orientation. You must see the pattern clearly before you can re-write it.

Orient: The Conscious Pivot of Power

This is your moment of power. Instead of Observe - Act, you PIVOT TO ORIENT. You take the data from your Observation and you pause. You ask yourself:

"Given what I've Observed, what do I intend to create now?"

"What is my desired outcome?"

"What is the 'seed' I want to sow?"

Tool for Orientation: 10 Minutes of Boredom

In our over-stimulated world, we must intentionally create the space for Orientation.

As the author Jay Shetty recommends, practicing 10 minutes

of boredom each day—no phone, no book, no distraction—is a powerful reset.

It calms the reactive mind and creates the quiet internal space necessary for you to consciously Orient.

Act: The Expression of Energy

Having chosen your Orientation, you now Act. This is often the hardest part, where inertia and procrastination stop us.

The solution is to remember: momentum comes before motivation.

You don't "wait" to feel motivated. You Act in a small way to create motivation.

Tools for Action:

Perfection Never Delivers: The goal is not a perfect Act, but a started Act.

The 5-Minute Rule: Choose the one task you are resisting. Give yourself permission to do it for only 5 minutes.

The Zigarnik Effect: This small "Act" leverages a powerful brain quirk. Your brain hates unfinished tasks and will naturally want to complete them once you've started. That 5-minute start is often all it takes to break the inertia.

Realise: The Present-Moment Integration

The moment you Act, the universe provides immediate feedback.

Realise is the act of accepting and integrating this new reality in the present moment.

You send a calm, oriented message (your Act).

You Realise an immediate feeling of inner peace and self-respect, regardless of the reply. That feeling is the new Quan.

The "two-point life" ignores this step. It bypasses the feeling of the new reality and looks only for the external result, missing the harvest of its own creation.

Reflect: The Spiral of Integration & Your Internal Mentor

This is the final, vital phase in the cycle of any OOARR Infinity Loop, whether it is momentary, weekly, monthly, annually, whatever the fractal of time. Reflect is the cognitive review of the harvest. It is the act of consciously analyzing the outcome of your loop to evolve your consciousness. This is where you learn.

You ask:

"What worked? What didn't? Why?"

"How will I adjust my 80% practice for the next loop?"

Tool for Reflection: Reward Effort

This is also reward time.

To make the loop sustainable, you must reward effort, not outcomes.

At the end of your day, Reflect on 3 things you achieved—even if it was just "I successfully used the 5-minute rule."

This conscious reward generates dopamine, reinforces the new neural pathway, and makes the loop desirable to your brain.

The wisdom you gain from your Reflection becomes the new foundation for your next Observation. You are no longer solving the same problem. Your Observations themselves are evolving. You are spiraling up to a higher, more coherent level of creation.

Becoming Your Own Mentor: The "Reflect" Loop

This is why the Reflect phase can be your most self-empowering step of the entire practice.

When you lack an external mentor, the "Reflect" loop becomes your internal mentor.

I know this personally. Early in my life, I qualified for both Medicine and Engineering. I had no one around to help me Observe my own nature, my inclination to deeper human interactions. Lacking that mentor, I chose the process engineering path because it seemed to be aligned with my continuing concern and interest in our global environment .

Later, I actively tried to enlist a mentor. My inclinations to deeper things manifest as political aspirations. In the early '80s Marg and I used to be invited to join our friend, Claude Faye, who was a leading Perth entrepreneur, on his classic Halvorsen boat for afternoon cruises on the Swan River in Perth.

At least a couple of those times Claude's very good friend, Fred Chaney, the Leader of the Senate in Australia at the time, would also be invited to join the afternoon cruise. On one of these occasions, I took the opportunity (my Act) to ask Fred to mentor me considering my interest in politics. He never took it up. Undoubtedly Fred was just too busy.

It occurs to me now, almost forty five years later, that Claude, ever the gentleman, was a real mentor to me. He could have invited so many people out on that boat besides twenty somethings, John and Marg. Who knows, he could have invited Fred along with us because he saw political potential in me or Marg.

In December 1988, years after I finished working with him, Claude invited me to lunch with him at "Sorrento" a renowned Italian restaurant which was one of the go to spots in Perth, Western Australia in the 80s. In typical gracious Claude fashion, he observed me eating spaghetti incorrectly and then, very kindly, showed me how to eat spaghetti correctly, winding it with my fork.

At that lunch Claude encouraged me to catch up with him to explore what we could do together after I returned from my long awaited Round-the-World in (almost) 80 Days adventures with Marg and our then young children, Adam, who was 6 1/2 at the time, Brett who was almost 5 and Jess who was almost 3 1/2.

It was to be a journey filled with awe, including: white water rafting down the Zambezi; sitting with the kids in front of the Mona Lisa (while Adam was repeatedly saying "sortie, sortie" "the exit, the exit"); being amazed by The Roquettes at Radio City Music Hall and Christmas in New York; beholding the Na Pali Coast, the cliffs on the northwest shore of Kauai, Hawaii.

Remembering this was pre-mobile phones and faxes were the most advanced communications technology. Immediately on my return I called for Claude. I cannot recall whether I spoke to Claude's lovely wife Bridget - I was informed Claude had died suddenly

He was only in his early forties - more than twenty years younger than I am now. He was the grandson of Claude de Bernales who was both a "colourful entrepreneur" way before Alan Bond and, like Bond, of Americas Cup sailing renowned, de Bernales was transformative of Perth and the Western Australian gold industry in particular. His grandson, Claude Faye, was a young man of great integrity and resources. Who knows what worlds lay ahead for Claude and his beautiful family.

My experience with Fred Chaney and politics is an important lesson: You cannot force resonance. I resonated with Claude Faye but the universe had other ideas.

A mentor is part of the 20% "Let Them" field.

So, what do you do? You Observe your "sliding door

moments" (the Medicine/ Process Engineering choice).

You Orient to it with Self-Wonder ("I wonder what I can learn from this?").

You Realise what is now - your personal universe in this moment.

You Reflect, with AWE - Awareness Wonder Expectancy - on life from those youthful days to now. You integrate the wisdom.

You can become your own mentor in this way. Like me with my process engineering orientation, seeing the AWE and Infinity Loop processes, which I hope will be life enhancing for millions of people, in the deepest possible ways - you will see even more positively impactful possibilities that you can make real to the benefit of all.

PART 5 : POWER QUANTUM LEAPS IN YOUR LIFE

Quantum Leaps = ATOMIC Habits (OOARR Infinity Loops) To The Power Of (QUANTUM Habits)

There is a wonderful, global best selling book called "Atomic Habits" by James Clear.

"Atomic Habits" is an outstanding but Newtonian model of self-improvement.

You will see the benefit of adding AWE to this, enabling you to make Quantum Leaps.

"AWE" equips you for Quantum self-creation - engaging both of our "oars" : our quantum "oars" - AWE one Awareness Wonder Expectancy and OOARR two - Observe Orient Act Realise Reflect.

Atomic Habits , in this context of good habits creation, may be thought of as your "oar" two:

You Observe with Self AWE, You Orient, You Act, You Realise, You Reflect

The OOARR Loop is fractal, one loop at a time: one thought, one microsecond, one minute scaling fractally to one week, one year, one decade, one lifetime - compounding, as James Clear observes, over time (like compound interest).

Quantum Habits are energetic imagination. You begin with collapsing reality through your conscious, oriented observation.

Quantum Habits and Atomic Habits are not mutually exclusive

- I absolutely encourage you to use both Quantum and Atomic protocols

The Core Distinction between Atomic Habits and Quantum Habits is: Atomic is Doing while Quantum is Being

The AWE Framework for Quantum Habits

With the AWE Framework for Quantum Habits, you aren't just building a routine - you are engaging in Co-Creation with the Quantom - the infinite ocean of the universe of possibilities.

A - Awareness (The Multiworld Orientation)

Atomic View: "I am currently out of shape, so I will go to the gym." (Reacting to current fixed reality).

Quantum View: You become aware of the Multiworld

In the quantum field, there is already a version of you that is perfectly healthy, and a version that is unwell. Both exist as potentials in the Quantom dimensions.

The Quantum Habit: for fitness, for example, is not "racing to the gym" .... Just yet.

The Quantum habit is the mental discipline of holding Awareness of the desired self in the Multiworld, rather than defaulting to the observation of the current physical self.

W - Wonder (Connecting to the Quantom)

Atomic View: "I hope this works."

Quantum View:

This sounds surreal because Quantum Reality is surreal - You simply wonder

The Quantum Habit:

This is the emotional energetic charge. Instead of

"willpower" (which burns out), you use "Wonder."

You marvel at the version of you that already exists in the Quantom field - the universal ocean of possibilities..

This emotional signature is the reality magnet.

E - Expectancy (Collapsing Reality)

Atomic View: Waiting for results to prove the habit is working.

Quantum View: You collapse the wave function holding Expectancy. You drag that specific probability from the Multiworld into your Quan (personal reality).

The Quantum Habit is Acting from the end state.

You don't run to become a runner - you run because you are a runner.

The Critical Factor is remembering that Materiality creates Drag and Friction

This is the missing link that makes Quantum Habits reality rather than just magical thinking.

In the Quantom dimensions, manifestation is instant.

We live in a physical plane with materiality and density.

When you collapse a new reality, it must push through Materiality Drag Friction.

Quantum Leaps Escape Friction with Frequency, Imagination and Fun

Quantum Habits do not rely on repetitions.

Your personal Quantum Leaps start with your AWE - Awareness Wonder Expectancy - bringing your personal universe - your Quan - into harmony and alignment with the superposition of your wellbeing in the universe of infinite possibilities - the

Quantom

Atomic Habits reinforce your Quantum Leaps.

You engage your second "oar", Observe, Orient, Act, Realise, Reflect to counter friction you experience in life (your effort, repetition and discipline, sometimes through discomfort, grinding and even pain).

The "Drag" is not failure. Drag is just lag.

When you engage both of your "oars" , you will not see the physical result instantly (because of the drag).

An Atomic Habit approach says "Keep pushing."

A Quantum Habit approach says "Hold the frequency." If you drop the frequency (your resonance with the universe) because you don't see the result - you let doubt enter - the wave function un-collapses. "The double minded man will get nothing"

The Quantum Habit is the refusal to let physical friction dictate your quantum frequency.

Atomic Habits are about changing what you do now so that down the track - it may be in a few weeks or a year or more - you will change who you are.

Quantum Habits are about changing who you are now (in the Quantom)

By changing who you are now, what you do naturally aligns with your new reality.

THE QUANTOM WAY TO CHANGE WHO YOU ARE NOW IS WITH A WHOLE BRAIN HUDDLE

We need to use our two "oars" to navigate the infinite ocean of possibilities and to handle the time lag between the quantum shift and the physical manifestation. These two "oars" are virtually entirely in control of our brain. We need the "Whole Brain Huddle"

The "Whole Brain Huddle" conceived by Dr. Jill Bolte Taylor is the conscious, intentional act of bringing your entire inner crew to our boat - floating on the infinite ocean of possibilities.

We need our brain's left hemisphere Navigator (C1) and Primal Alarm (C2), and we need our brain's right hemisphere Sensory Anchor (C3) and Wise Visionary (C4) to connect and join the Huddle.

It's moving from the Newtonian Trap of the C2-C1 Nervous Navigator reactive spiral to a C1-C2-C3-C4 Whole Brain Huddle state of creative flow.

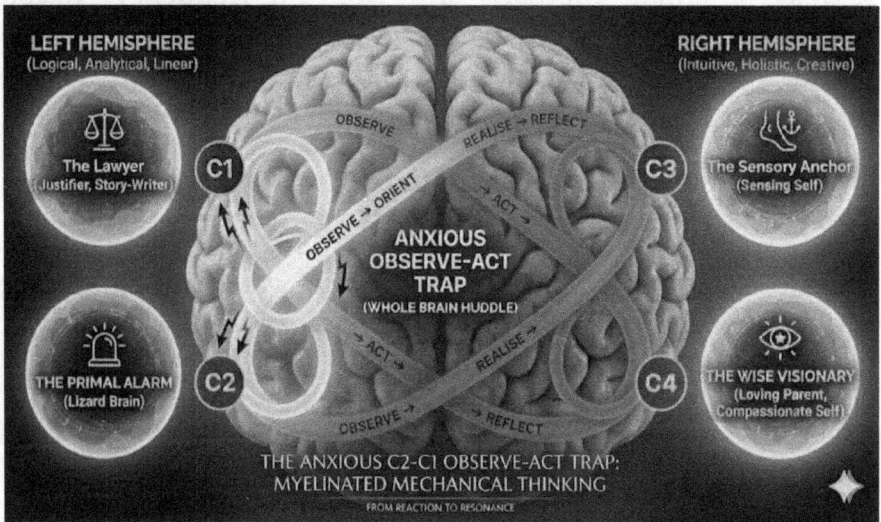

As the image here shows, we need our C3 Sensory Anchor to pull us out of the C1 -C2 Trap.

To do this we must engage all senses to help calm us and provide the 90 seconds we need to get the Whole Brain Huddle into action.

Training for the Pause: Tactics

We must be prepared. When the wave hits, we must have practiced our tactics and have our tactics ready, including simple sensory C3 engaging protocols such as:

Box Breathing: In for 4, hold for 4, out for 4, hold for 4.

The 5-4-3-2-1 Technique: Name 5 things you can see, 4 you can feel, 3 you can hear, 2 you can smell, 1 you can taste.

Name It: Simply say, "I am feeling the 90-second surge of 'My Primal Alarm'. I am not the surge."

Here is a very beautiful and powerful conceptual illustration of the transition through four brain states, displayed here in full colour in the printed book. As for all the images in this book, they are designed to be illustrative and empower awe. Note: some eBook devices display the images in grey scale.

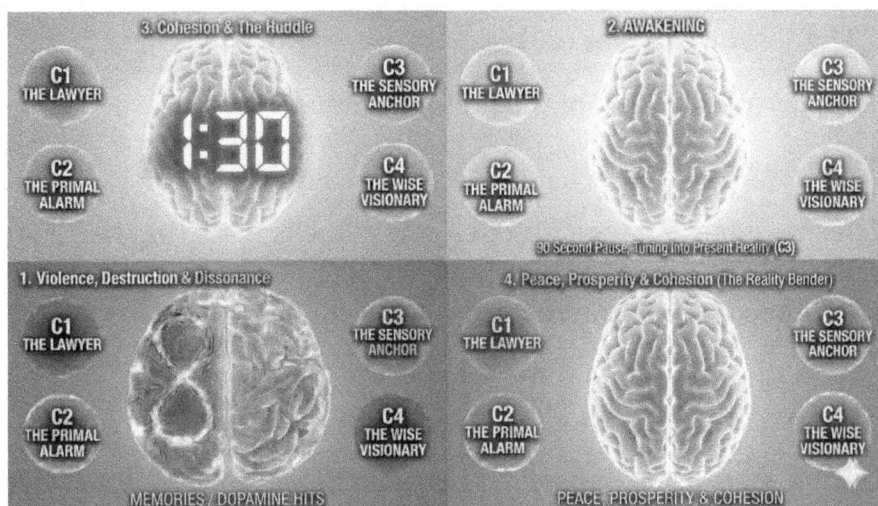

The image illustrates MOVING FROM DISSONANCE TO PEACE : COHERENCE AND CONSCIOUS CREATION by engaging all the crew in our beautiful and quantum powered brains

THE HUDDLE IN ITS PUREST

FORM: CHILD GENIUS

This "Huddle" is not a complex skill we need to learn; it's a natural state we must reclaim.

This is the "elevated huddle" I see in my granddaughter, Maddie.

The Storyteller (The Conscious Child):

When Maddie plays, she is "singing and telling stories out loud... as she plays."

This isn't idle chatter; it's the sound of a universe being built in real-time.

Her inner monologue is spoken aloud. She is seamlessly fusing:

o The Visionary Wise Self (C4):

The imaginative, big-picture vision of the game.

o The Sensory Anchor (C3):

The playful "wonder" of the present moment.

o The Navigator (C1):

The language and logic to tell a story. She is narrating her own reality as she creates it. Her thoughts, words, and actions are one simultaneous, integrated flow.

The Seer (The Present Moment Connector)

During storytime, I observed her stop listening, look up at her Nana (my wife, Marg), and say,

"I'm looking into your eyes."

In that moment, she elevated the entire experience.

Maddie realized the most important thing wasn't the content

(the book); it was the connection.

Maddie was practicing pure Observation (Awareness).

Maddie was embodying The Sensory Anchor (C3), feeling the present-moment connection.

Maddie was demonstrating The Visionary Wise Self (C4), understanding that love and connection are the "real event" beyond the words.

Reclaiming the Child Huddle: Reflective Prompts for Adults

As adults, we must consciously practice what a child does instinctively.

We can use simple, reflective prompts.

To Activate "The Storyteller":

o Core Prompt:

"What story am I narrating for myself right now?"

o The Action Prompt:

"How can I shift my narration from reacting to this moment to composing it?"

To Activate "The Seer"

o Core Prompt:

"Am I just looking at this, or am I truly seeing it?"

o The Action Prompt:

"What is the real event happening here, beyond the content and the words?"

THE ARCHITECTURAL HUDDLE: MANIFESTING VISION IN STONE AND STEEL

If a child's play is the Huddle in its purest form, great architecture is the Huddle in a most physical, high-stakes form.

The architect must be both a Visionary Self (C4) architect and a Navigator/ Justifier (C1) negotiator and master of physics.

Architect, Frank Gehry designer of the
Walt Disney Concert Hall in LA

I was in LA in 2016 at one of those classic old theaters. It was a fireside chat guided by Brian Chesky, one of the founders of Airbnb and Frank Gehry.

I was fortunate to be in the front row. Brian asks Frank about his creative moment which led to the Walt Disney Concert Hall in LA.

Gehry starts crumpling an A4 piece of paper - a pure Sensory Anchor (C3) "playful" and Visionary Self (C4) "visionary" act.

He intentionally bypasses his Navigator (C1), which would give him a boring box.

His C4 vision was so powerful, his C1 "Navigator/ Justifier" had to seek new technology (adapting aerospace software CATIA) just to make the C4 vision real.

Jørn Utzon (Sydney Opera House)

This is the story of a C4 vision colliding with a C1 world.

Utzon's C4 vision (the "sails") was so far ahead of its time that the collective Navigator (C1) of the engineers and politicians broke down.

They fell into a C1-led "Zeno Trap" of budgets and "it-can't-be-done" logic.

The Opera House stands as a testament to a C4 vision so powerful it survived the breakdown of the Huddle.

MODELS OF GENIUS: THE "HUDDLE" VS. THE "CHANNEL"

The Whole Brain Huddle (Leonardo da Vinci):

Leonardo is the archetype of the Whole Brain Huddle.

His Sensory Anchor (C3) was filled with childlike wonder:

"How does a bird fly?"

His Navigator (C1) was the logical servant to that wonder

"Let's find out" by dissecting the bird.

The Mona Lisa is the result, in part, of his C1 scientific knowledge of anatomy and optics being used to express a C4 vision of human essence.

The Channel (Jackson Pollock & Pablo Picasso)

This is another kind of genius.

This is the act of intentionally silencing the C1 and C2 to become a pure conduit for C3 and C4.

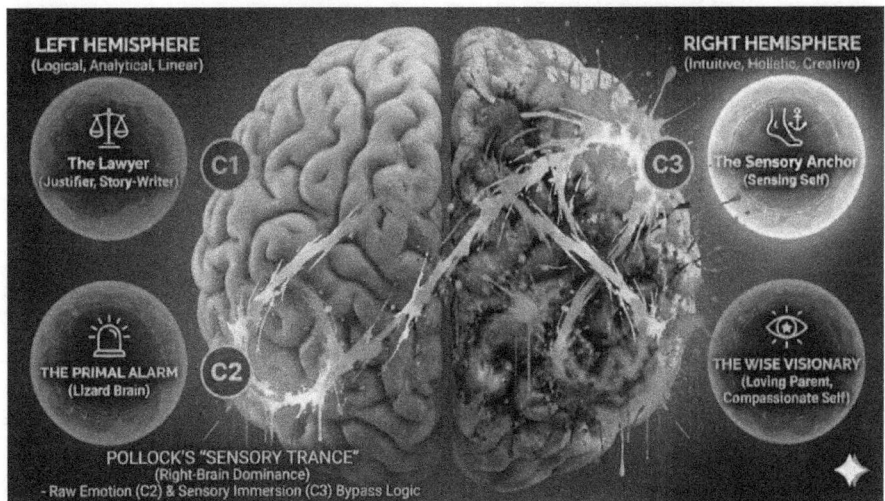

LEFT HEMISPHERE (Logical, Analytical, Linear)

RIGHT HEMISPHERE (Intuitive, Holistic, Creative)

The Lawyer (Justifier, Story-Writer) C1

C3 The Sensory Anchor (Sensing Self)

THE PRIMAL ALARM (Lizard Brain) C2

THE WISE VISIONARY (Loving Parent, Compassionate Self)

POLLOCK'S "SENSORY TRANCE" (Right-Brain Dominance) - Raw Emotion (C2) & Sensory Immersion (C3) Bypass Logic

The Image here is my favourite image in the book. It is very much in the style of Pollock. Flashes of wild brilliance. It illustrates The C2/C3 Channel Brain of Jackson Pollock. This is where YOU will have to use your imagination in a C3 dominant way.

Jackson Pollock was a C3-dominant creator. His "action painting" was a C3-led dance, a state of pure, non-judgmental "being in the painting."He said,

"The painting has a life of its own. I try to let it come through."

Pablo Picasso was a C1 master who chose to paint like a C3 child.

He famously said,

"It took me four years to paint like Raphael, but a lifetime to paint like a child."

Like our 3 year old granddaughter Maddie, Frank Gehry and Leonardo da Vinci, Pablo Picasso wilfully shattered the C1 logical view of reality to show you a C4 "big picture" (all angles at once), expressed with the raw, present-moment energy of The Sensory Anchor (C3).

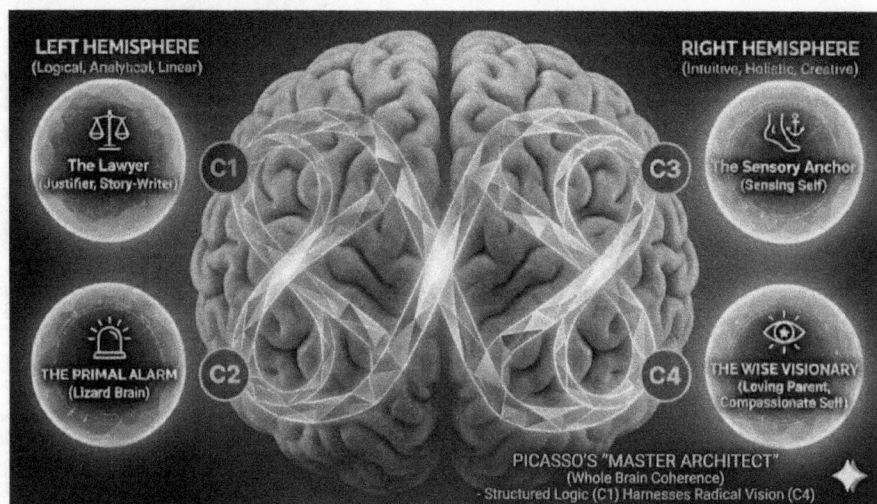

THE HIGH-STAKES HUDDLE: FROM ZENO TRAP TO QUANTUM RESONANCE

For decades, I lived in a Newtonian world of "cause and effect."

If I wanted a different result, I believed I had to "push" harder.

This is the "unconscious creation" of the reactive brain.

What we are all waking up to is that we are not just mechanical reactors.

We are Quantum resonators.

We don't just react to the world; we resonate with a field of potential (the Quantom) to co-create our reality (our Quan).

The 90-second pause is the key that unlocks this shift, especially in high-stakes moments, like pitching a revolutionary idea.

This is what the reactive brain does before a big pitch.

The Primal Alarm (C2) Hijacks the Meeting:

Before I even walk in, my C2 flares up: "Who are you to be in this room?" "These people are out of your league." "Don't embarrass yourself."

The Navigator (C1) Springs the "Zeno Trap":

My logical C1 sees this C2 fear and desperately tries to "solve" it. It goes into overdrive, rehearsing the opening line 100 times and creating 10 backup PowerPoint presentations.

This is the Zeno Trap: you are so busy analyzing the thousand tiny steps to 'not failing' that you completely disconnect from the original, creative spark.

In 1989, while I was a self-funded student doing my Masters majoring in Innovation at UWA, I sent a very detailed business plan (part of which I also submitted as an assignment on marginal pricing) for a new airline in Australia to Sir Richard Branson.

His CEO wrote back, proposing to meet me in London to discuss this plan.

I felt (Observed) I was in this trap.

I was a "student" running my own process engineering firm, with a "young family."

My Navigator (C1) told me I didn't have the money nor the time available to head off to London. My Primal Alarm (C2) reminded me of my childhood of some lack - you do not want your children to experience that. My C1 and C2 created a Zeno Trap.

Conceivably this may have been one of the great opportunities of my life time - missed by not allowing my Wise Visionary, my C4, to huddle with my C3, Sensory Anchor and not leave out my C1, C2 - have whole brain huddle and figure out a way. The obvious - now - would have been to ask Virgin to cover my costs! If they said "No" then they would not have been seriously interested.

This was decades before Sir Richard Branson's friend and my friendly acquaintance, Bill Tai, seed funded Zoom. There were no video calls.

The pitch never happened.

Virgin Australia first launched in Australia 10 years later on August 31, 2000 as Virgin Blue. .

This was at the time that I was launching Hypertrade. A platform to connect clients of global accounting firms with the vision to enable these validated companies and organizations to connect and transact online with each other.

I did get to pitch in London and Baltimore. This time my

pitch was successful. Hypertrade (trading on the ASX as Gold Partners) became an Australian darling of the early internet boom. Unfortunately Hypertrade was a casualty of the 2002 internet crash. It was a great idea. It is still a great idea.

I did have the privilege of meeting Sir Richard on Necker Island, where he lives , at the time, with his lovely wife Joan. This was for a start up event organised by Bill Tai.

I was talking to Joan about how much I enjoyed kite surfing from the beach on the island.

I will always remember, in the Necker Island beach hut, there was (likely is still) a lovely photo of William and Harry as kids on the beach there with their mum, Diana.

Joan told me that Richard had hurt himself launching his kite off the beach there just recently.

I said to Joan, "You know a lot about Richard".

She replied, "I should, he's my husband".

I laughed out loud as Sir Richard approached and joined us both.

I had no idea I'd been in a very engaged conversation with Sir Richard's lovely wife. In fact when Sir Richard first arrived into his very large bar / entertaining area I happened to walk by him, both of us smiling and saying "hi" to each other, with two pina coladas, one for me and one for Joan.

A Personal Aside : Vale Joan Templeman

More than a month after I originally recounted this reflection of mine in writing this book, I come back to this story on 26 November 2025, the day I learned of Joan's passing.

Richard reflected on their "incredible" their lives together:

"Joan was my everything, the shining star around which our family's

universe has always orbited.

That light is not gone; it's just taken on a new shape. It will guide us forward. And we will carry her with us, always"

I never saw the opportunity on Necker to ask Sir Richard if he remembered my business plan of a quarter of century prior and the idea to meet his Virgin CEO in London.

Maybe Sir Richard will listen to this as an audiobook and let me know. In this case, "Hopefully Sir Richard you will think this book contains wisdom".

THE 90-SECOND PAUSE: IGNITING THE "WHOLE BRAIN HUDDLE"

Back to pitching or any important conversation (almost all conversations are important).

This is the Whole Brain Huddle you run before big conversations, presentations, meetings or announcements.

Like the Whole Brain Huddle I am having right now with myself about the potential importance and significance of this book,"AWE, Now Consciously Create Your Personal Universe"

STOP (The Circuit-Break):

You feel the Primal Alarm C2 adrenaline.

You're tempted to run your Navigator C1 notes or thinking one last time.

Don't.

Pause.

Observe the chatter without judgment.

TUNE in by using your first "oar" , Awareness Wonder

Expectancy with the help of:

➤ The Sensory Anchor C3:

Get present

Feel your feet on the floor.

Take a physiological sigh (a deep breath in, a sip more, a slow breath out)

You are here, now.

➤ The Visionary Wise Self C4:

Connect to the wider universe (the Quantom).

What is the highest potential for this?

Connect with the core purpose of your idea—the excitement, the service it provides, the solution it offers, the wisdom.

Feel the Expectancy of that positive outcome.

Now for CREATE , engage your "oar" two, Observe Orient Act Realise Reflect requires :

➤ Your Visionary Self (C4). Your Wise Visionary holds the inspiring vision (the "Why").

➤ It passes this calm, confident energy to your Navigator (C1).

Your C1's job is no longer "How do I not fail?"

Its new job is

"How do I clearly communicate this amazing vision?"

➤ Your Sensory Anchor (C3) adds passion and charisma, allowing you to connect with people as fellow humans.

➤ Your Primal Alarm (C2) is still there, but C4 has its hand on C2's shoulder.

Fear is just data, not a directive.

When you move forward, your entire energetic signature has changed.

You are no longer a Newtonian reactor.

You are a Quantum resonator, calm, present, and vibrating with the full, coherent potential of your idea.

THE C2-C1 MYELINATED NEWTONIAN TRAP : VIOLENCE, ADDICTIONS, PSYCHOSES

Now let's consider the shadow sides of we humans, a lot of which is within our 80% control.

The "Hijack": Understanding the C2-C1 "Skewed Thinking" Trap

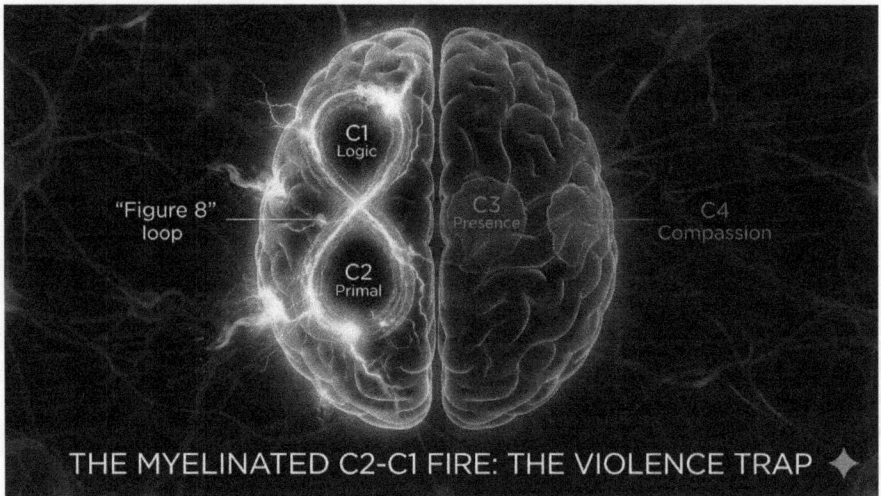

THE MYELINATED C2-C1 FIRE: THE VIOLENCE TRAP

Wars, Domestic Violence, Rage, Addictions and Psychoses, are where the C2-C1 Newtonian Trap are at its most dangerous.

Psychosis was, sadly, my mother's experience, at intervals, sometimes frequent, in her life. A perceived reality born from her thought processes and genetics, not any external substance. The violence involved was entirely personal to her. We children were in fear (and awe) of the terror which was evident in her eyes. This shadow side, this 20% genetic "Given" was so present and strong.

Imagine, in a moment of stress or exhaustion, your mind produces an image so terrifying it feels utterly real. You imagine you are seeing and experiencing the devil.

This isn't a metaphor. It's a full-blown sensory and emotional experience. This is a "skewed thinking" loop.

The Primal Alarm (C2) Hijacks Reality:

Your C2—the storehouse of all your deepest, oldest, and most profound fears and traumas—erupts.

It projects this terrifying holograph as a "truth." This is the Observe.

The Navigator (C1) Springs the "Zeno Trap":

Your logical C1 sees this C2 hijack and, in a desperate panic, tries to "solve" it. Its logic is now poisoned.

It doesn't ask, "Am I safe?"

It asks, "What did I do to deserve this?" "Is this real?" "Am I being punished?" "Am I evil?" "Am I going insane?"

The Downward Spiral: This is the stuck loop.

o Your Primal Alarm C2 (Fear) provides the terrifying data:

"DANGER! THE DEVIL!"

o Your Navigator C1 (Logic) analyses this data and "confirms" it:

"This is terrifying, therefore it must be real.

If it's real, I am doomed."

o This logical "confirmation" (the Act) feeds more terror back into your Primal Alarm C2.

o C2 erupts even stronger, providing "more evidence" for your Navigator C1.

This is a closed, deterministic Newtonian Trap C2-C1 spiral. You are completely disembodied (no Sensory Anchor C3) and utterly disconnected from your compassionate higher self (no Wise Visionary C4).

The 90-Second Pause: The "Whole Brain Huddle" Lifeline

This terrifying moment is the most critical time for the 90-second pause. It applies to any situation where you find yourself in the Newtonian Trap of your mind's C1-C2 loop.

STOP (The Circuit-Break):

You are in the experience.

The temptation is to fight it or engage with it (your Navigator C1 analysis). Don't.

Pause.

Find the part of you that can Observe the experience without becoming it.

"I am observing a feeling of terror. I am observing a terrifying presence"

TUNE (The AWE Input):

You now must manually activate your Right Brain (Sensory Anchor C3 and Wise Visionary C4). It will not activate automatically under these conditions.

o The Sensory Anchor (C3):

This is your anchor to the real reality.

Force it.

Name five things you can see in the room.

The lamp. The book. The carpet. The TV. The glass

Feel your feet on the floor.

These are the anti-psychosis acts

They prove you are in a body, in a room, not in the C2-generated nightmare.

o The Visionary Wise Self (C4):

This is the call for grace.

Ask, "What is the highest potential for this moment?"

The answer is peace and safety.

Your Visionary Self (C4) is the part of you that is already whole and safe.

It's the loving and wise parent that looks at the terrified Primal Alarm C2 and says,

"I see you. You are terrified. But that is not you. That is a feeling. You are safe. I am here."

CREATE (The OOARR Huddle), engage your "oar" two, Observe Orient Act Realise Reflect:

Your Visionary Self (C4) holds the loving vision of safety.

Your Sensory Anchor (C3) holds you in the present, physical moment.

They pass this energy to your Navigator (C1), giving it a new, life-saving job.

Your Navigator C1's new job: "How do I align with the truth that I am safe?"

Your Sensory Anchor C3 provides the action: "Let's take one, single, deep breath."

Your Wise Visionary C4 provides the compassion: "You are okay. This is just a powerful, old energy moving through. Let it go."

The Primal Alarm (C2) is still screaming.

But it's no longer driving the car.

C4 has its hand on C2's shoulder.

The "devil" (whatever or whoever that "devil" is) is seen for what it is: not an external entity, but the symbolic representation of your C2's deepest pain, finally coming to the surface to be healed by C4's compassion.

Personal Aside

I wish my beautiful, gracious Mum was still alive and I could share these insights with her and see if they resonated for her and whether they could help her.

Hopefully they help many, many others. Mum would love this to be the case. She was so loving and caring. Her "We" orientation was very active.

2006 WORLD CUP FINAL : ZIDANE'S HEADBUTT

This C2-C1 hijack is the "red mist" in sports. It's the source of "skewed thinking" that costs games.

The "Huddle" is the tool to break it.

I decided to include these sports metaphors ahead of the next series of applications of the "Huddle" and the Self AWE / O-O-A-R-R processes to provide relatable and memorable stories, to make it easier to apply in day-to-day life.

The Soccer (Football) Real Life Zinedine Zidane "Red Mist" Moment

One of the most famous "Red Mist" moments in history: Zinedine Zidane's headbutt in the 2006 World Cup Final.

It was Zinedine Zidane's final game. He was a master.

A Primal Alarm C2 trigger (an insult) hijacked his Wise Visionary C4 legacy. He reacted (Newtonian) rather than paused (Quantum).

That one second of lost coherence cost a World Cup.

This illustrates the high stakes of the "90-second pause" better than any generic example.

Here is a fuller story of that infamously expensive moment, retold through the lens of the Primal Alarm versus the Wise Visionary.

The 110th Minute: When the Visionary Blinked

Berlin, July 9, 2006. The World Cup Final.

Zinedine Zidane is not just a player in this game; he is the conductor. It is the final match of his career. He has already scored a Panenka penalty—a chip so audacious, so calm, it signaled to the world that he was operating on a higher plane of consciousness. He is fully embodying the Wise Visionary. He is leading his nation. He is ten minutes from a penalty shootout that France is favored to win.

Fatigue is setting in. The air is thick. The tension is palpable.

Marco Materazzi, the Italian defender, is doing what he does best: nagging, pulling, provoking. He grabs Zidane's jersey. It's annoying, but manageable.

Zidane, still in his Wise Visionary C4 state, offers a sarcastic, witty retort: "If you want my shirt so badly, I'll give it to you after the match."

It was a verbal parry—controlled, superior, calm.

Then, Materazzi mumbles the trigger. He insults Zidane's sister.

The Hijack

In a split second, the atmosphere shifts. The roar of 69,000 fans fades into a dull hum. Zidane's peripheral vision collapses. The Wise Visionary C4—the part of him concerned with legacy, with the team, with the World Cup trophy standing just yards away—is aggressively shoved aside.

Zidane's Primal Alarm C2 screams.

This is the Red Mist. It is a biological takeover. A surge of cortisol and adrenaline floods his system, designed for one thing only: defending the tribe. Insulting his family registers not as words, but as a physical threat.

The Newtonian Reaction

Zidane stops. He turns. There is no Quantum Pause. There is no gap between stimulus and response. He does not observe the feeling; he becomes the feeling.

He becomes a predictable object in a Newtonian universe: Action (Insult) : Reaction (Violence).

He lowers his head and drives it into Materazzi's chest.

It wasn't a fight; it was an execution. It was the C2 Alarm hitting the emergency brake on the C4 Visionary's destiny.

The Cost of Lost Coherence

The referee's whistle blows. The red card is raised.

The image that follows is haunting: Zidane walks off the pitch, head bowed, undoing the tape on his wrists. He passed the solid gold World Cup trophy. He doesn't look at it. He can't. He has just exiled himself from the celebration he was building.

France loses the penalty shootout. The greatest player of his generation ends his career in a locker room, alone, listening to the muffled cheers of the Italians.

The Post Game Analysis: The 90-Second Rule

This national sporting catastrophe illustrates exactly why what I call the Quantum Algorithm (your AWE one and your OOARR two , with your entire crew working together in a Whole Brain Huddle) is essential at every moment of our lives. Lapses can cost so much.

The Failure: The hijack was total. Zidane lost "Coherence"—the alignment between his heart (passion) and brain (logic).

The Missing Step: If Zidane had engaged a 90-second pause, the chemical surge of the Red Mist would have flushed out of his system. The C2 Alarm would have quieted, allowing the C4 Visionary to come back online.

The Result: A paused Zidane would have laughed, pointed at

the scoreboard, and won the World Cup. A reactive Zidane lost everything in one second.

The Lesson

You are never more than one second away from losing your legacy to your biology. The Pause is not just a relaxation technique. It is a legacy protection mechanism.

NATIONAL & GLOBAL CONFLICTS :
THE PATH TO COHESION

The C2-C1 Newtonian Trap spiral of violence in the home is a microcosm.

The same tragic, "Newtonian" mechanism that very wrongly results in a man harming his partner, domestic violence, is what drives national division and nations to war.

The 2025 conflicts in Gaza, Israel, Ukraine, Thailand, Cambodia, Myanmar, Venezuela, The Congo and Sudan are not just political or territorial. They are the C2-C1 trap scaled to the collective.

They are the catastrophic outcome of millions of personal universes (Quans) clashing in a storm of dissonance.

Consider national and global conflicts.

A nation's Primal Alarm (C2) erupts, fueled by generations of historical trauma, real or perceived injustice, and a primal fear of "the other."

Instantly, the nation's Navigator / Justifier (C1)—especially its leader, and also its politicians, its media, its ideologues—get to work. The leader and the other Justifiers build a "logical" case for that primal fear. They find "evidence" for why the "other" is a threat, why the others are in the wrong, and why dominance or violence is the only "solution."

The Justifier's story is rocket fuel for the nation's Primal C2 rage.

In this state, The Sensory Anchor (C3) is offline.

These nations are no longer in the present reality.

They become lost in their Primal C2-generated story of past grievance and future threat.

And The Wise Visionary Self (C4) is completely silenced - often jailed or, in Putinesque and Kim Jong Un style, murdered.

Compassion for "the other" is seen as treason.

Empathy is reframed as "weakness."

The shared humanity of the "enemy" is erased.

The result is a deterministic spiral.

"Observe" (We are being attacked!) : "Act" (We must strike back!)

This act proves to the other side that their Primal C2 was right, and their C1 justifies their escalation.

It is the C2-C1 trap in a feedback loop of mutually assured destruction which has been going on in the Middle East for thousands of years.

The Path to Cohesion

Observation: The First Act of Creation

This state of AWE is the key that unlocks the door. How do you walk through it? Whether at the personal, interpersonal, community, national, international - as we have explored, these are fractals of each other.

So, whether at home or with warring nations, you continue with the next step of the active process of conscious creation: Observation.

You cannot change what you do not see. But if you try to observe your life from your "default mode," you will only see your old stories, your justifications, and your limitations.

To truly Observe—to see your unconscious personal universe as it is.

Throughout this book, we have journeyed together through this entire process.

We have learned to seek AWE (Awareness, Wonder, Expectancy) . Then we should not only Observe, take Pause so as to Orient well. Then take inspired Action, to Realise new possibilities in the present moment, and to Reflect on the new reality we are creating.

Our "OOARR" two is a fractal process and an infinite loop, extending before and beyond lifetimes.

"OOARR" two can occur in an instant, from Observation, Orientation, Action, Realisation, Reflection (with Reflection returning us instantly to Re-Observation, Re-orientation, Action (not reaction), Realisation, Reflection.

You will discover that once you have engaged AWE to quiet the "Nervous Navigator" and step out of your default programming. You have opened your senses. You are now in the clear, potent state of Observation.

For the first time, perhaps, you can see your personal universe—your previously unconscious Quan—with true clarity, without the fog of old judgments.

More importantly, you have stood at the shore of your own mind.

You have glimpsed that vast ocean of infinite potential, the Quantom. You, and you are no longer just an observer, but a participant.

You can see what is: You can sense what could be.

FROM GLOBAL TO EVERYDAY LIFE : THE 90-SECOND HIJACK (THE REPAIR LOOP)

This practice is messy. If you cannot handle the day-to-day, mundane moments of life, how could we ever imagine ourselves handling moments that are more personally or even universally vital, like those handled by Jesus, Churchill, Kennedy and Mandela.

Being aware and conscious of the 80/20 Rhythm of life demands we be honest about our "20%" hijack moments.

I experienced a classic, ever so mundane, hijack moment just the other day. Even though it was very mundane, it is not a huge leap to imagine a similar scenario, with other players, spiralling down into serious relational encounters or worse.

My wife, Marg, and I were in the car, which had just been re-gassed for air-conditioning. I turned on the air-con, and it blew hot air.

The Hijack (The Downward Spiral)

Observe: The air is hot

The Hijack (Primal Alarm): My Primal Alarm (C2) immediately triggered. I was "fuming." This was the 90-second chemical rush.

The Story (Justifier): I didn't let the 90-second wave pass. My Navigator (C1) built a story: "Somehow the service wasn't done, or it wasn't done correctly."

Dissonant Orient: My Orientation was now locked into this "fuming," "I've-been-wronged" state.

Dissonant Act: Marg rang the mechanic, Tom. She was phone-shy, so I took the phone. I thought I was being rational, but my frequency was accusatory.

Dissonant Realise: Tom Observed my frequency, which triggered his Primal Alarm. He "bit back," asking if I was suggesting he'd cheated me. We were in a reactive, dissonant loop.

The Repair (The Upward Spiral)

This is where practice really matters. I drove directly there, still "fuming."

Observe (New Data): Tom checked the car. It turned out the gas had leaked. A valve had released the gas overnight.

The Conscious Pivot (Orient): This new Observation shattered my Justifier's story. I instantly and consciously Pivoted to Orient. I let go of "fuming" and chose a new, coherent Orientation of "humility."

Coherent Act: I apologized.

Coherent Realise: The dissonance broke. Tom accepted my apology.

Coherent Act (Part 2): I apologized again to be sure.

Coherent Realise (An Upward Spiral): He accepted again, and then he apologized for "having a go" at me.

This is the 80/20 Rhythm in real-time. I "failed" the 90-second pivot. But because I was aware of the practice, I was able to use the next Observation to Re-Orient, Act coherently, and turn a Downward Spiral into an Upward Spiral. This is not about being perfect. It is about getting faster at the "repair loop."

This 5-stage Infinity Loop practice (Observe Orient Act Realise Reflect) is a perfect fractal that operates at every scale, from a single moment to a multi-year goal.

The "art" of this practice—the daily application, effectively dedicated training—is what builds conscious competence.

This includes protecting your first and last waking hour to consciously set your Orientation for the day and Reflect on it at night.

I fully expect some to read this and feel their own Primal Alarm (C2) go off. "How dare he!"

Their Navigator (C1) will immediately spring to action:

"This is disgustingly simplistic. He is comparing a complex geopolitical war to a domestic dispute. He is naive. He is dangerous. He is insulting the victims."

Ironically, that very reaction reveals the pathway to the solution.

That flash of Primal outrage (C2) and the "logical" case-building Navigator (C1) is the trap in action.

It proves how automatic, how myelinated, this C2-C1 spiral can become in any of us. This is how the spiral of domestic violence can be myelinated - locked in as an automatic reaction process.

The solution is not to deny our Primal C2 rage or our

NavigatorC1 logic.

The solution is to do the courageous work of bringing the other two parts of our brain to the table.

This is the "Whole Brain Huddle" on personal, community, national and global scales.

It is the 90-second lifeline for a leader, diplomat, politician, soldier, citizen, family, couple, you, me.

STOP.

Feel the Primal C2 (outrage).

Recognise the Navigator C1 (justification) for what it is.

Pause.

TUNE.

Bring The Sensory Anchor (C3) online.

What is the actual, present-moment reality, separate from my Primal C2-story about it?

TUNE.

Bring The Visionary Wise Self (C4) online.

What is the highest potential for this moment?

What action leads to safety and peace for everyone, not just "my side"?

CREATE.

Give The Navigator (C1) a new job.

Its job is no longer "How do we win?"

Its new, life-saving job is:

"Given our Primal C2 fear and our Visionary C4 goal of safety, what is the wisest plan of action right now?"

This is how our personal universes (Quans) can begin to coalesce in harmony rather than clash in dissonance.

John Lennon's anthem is not a naive dream. It is a Wise Visionary C4-led instruction.

To "live as one" is bringing (OOARR two) in action, synchronisation and resonance which harmonises with Awareness, Wonder, Expectancies (AWE one)

Well led Nations engaging in a global "Whole Brain Huddle"

Peace begins not in a peace treaty. Peace begins in the ninety seconds within each of our minds, as we orient to de-myelinate violence - not re-stimulate with hateful rhetoric, revisiting old narratives, creating and promoting conspiracy theories.

With a philosophy of do unto others as we would have them do unto us - and consciously myelinate for safety. We energise love. We can not only imagine, we can be among and enjoy:

" all the people livin' life in peace"

THE QUANTUM ALGORITHM
IN NORMAL LIFE
THE 50-YEAR REUNION

You have now Observed how patterns of coherence and dissonance show up in a number of historical situations, personal and sporting scenarios.

What happens when you face a pattern of dissonance in your own life or community? How do you actively change it?

The most powerful way to explain this is a real-world example.

This is the story of my 50 year school reunion in 2025. It is a wonderful example of how a group can use their natural goodwill to transform a legacy of dissonance into a new, coherent reality.

I went to Marist Brothers Eastwood in Sydney and I am proud to have been school captain there in 1975. In 2025, as the 50-year anniversary of our graduation from high school approached, a good friend from school, Ron Mees, called and asked me:

"Are we doing anything?"

This was a complex question.

Observe: Seeing the Full Picture

The first step is to have Awareness and Observe the reality as it truly is, without judgment.

When I looked back at our school, I saw a legacy of both

profound coherence and deep, painful dissonance.

The Coherence:

We had a great team and school spirit.

Men like our sports master, Ray Maguire, an Olympic boxer, and his assistant, Johnny Barber, a first-grade rugby league player led this. They were icons.

The Dissonance: This was mixed with deep dissonance.

One of our teachers, Michael Clohessy, bravely came out as gay on national television, on "A Current Affair" with Mike Willesee.

Today there may be a strong feeling of pride and unity about this, but then the Catholic Education system quickly dismissed him.

I had taken French in his class (we noted at our 50 year school reunion that Michael's name was "deleted" with that old-school white-out marker, on all end-of-year programs - one by one- by hand, as was the existence of the entire French class (also whited out).

The reality was at the time that there were quite a number of gay teachers and also a normal community level of gay students.

There was also a much darker shadow.

One of the brothers, who taught me as a 10 year old, Dacian, was subsequently convicted of crimes against children. I can recall him calling me out to the front of the class, ostensibly to congratulate me about something. He then tucked my shirt into my pants. In front of everyone in the class. I certainly was not the only one Dacian impacted. For a number of students these encounters were far worse.

This terrible dissonance had a significant impact on how many people perceived their time at the school.

This was the mixed reality: great pride alongside great pain. A lesser group might have just let the anniversary pass, focusing only on the "poor reflections" and the dissonance. Quite fairly a number of students, friends, from the time quite reasonably opted not to join in the reunion.

Orient: Setting the Intention

The next step was the Orient.

This is the conscious choice of direction.

Instead of focusing on the shadow, I—and the friends I spoke with—chose, due their good nature, not set practice, to orient toward the positive: the incredible team spirit, the lifelong bonds, and the pride we felt.

We aligned our internal state with the coherent memories.

To be clear, I did not discuss anything about my thoughts on consciously creating your personal universe to any of the boys, now men, I reached out to.

I and they shared wonder and expectancies of having a great time together, reminiscing on our times together and the future.

Act: Taking Conscious Action

The third step is to Act.

An orientation is just a thought until you do something.

I took it upon myself to reach out and "touch base."

I had very few contacts, literally just four or five. Remember we are from the pre-social media and the pre-mobile phone era. So even if I had everyone's telephone numbers, which I did not, they would be no longer existent dial up numbers

I used those contacts to find others, and they found others.

This was the conscious, creative Act to build new, fresh connections and community for our group.

Realise: Manifesting the New Reality

The fourth step is to Realise.

This is the present-moment integration, where your action becomes a new reality.

We ended up with over 40 people gathering in Moss Vale.

The moment we came together, we realised a new, powerful coherence. The spirit was wonderful.

The girls, the partners and wives, who came with their partners said they hadn't seen them "like this for so long," that they were "like children, so excited." Everyone, including the girls, had a wonderful mini weekend.

One of the girls who came is the widow of one of the 14 plus who have passed away. Why I say 14 plus is that I was not able to (yet) locate all the boys of the Class of '75/'73.

All the boys there, as almost 70 year olds, after our dinner event, joined in the school war cry in honour of those who had passed away.

I can tell you that more than a few tears were shed, not least by me.

In those moments we were not tied up in the poor reflections.

We were fully present in a new, joyful reality that we had created.

We realised the coherence that we had oriented toward.

Reflect: Learning and Integrating

The final step is to Reflect. This is the cognitive review of what happened.

My reflection, and the one that powers this section of the book, is this: Coherence from a group not only changes that group and its individuals.

It can change a whole community's perception of its history.

We didn't erase the dissonance of the past, but we created a new, more powerful coherent memory to define our legacy.

I was so happy to see the ripple effect. About three months later, the class of '70 held their own 55th-anniversary gathering and did the same.

Our group unconsciously engaged in the Quantum Algorithm to move forward to a new positive history to come. You can do the same in your school, community or family. You just have to be the one to pick up the oars and take the first stroke.

THE MORNING SWIM AT PREVELLY

We've seen how coherence and dissonance are inherited through families and how a group and hopefully families, couples and individuals can change their futures.

Now, let's scale this up to the communities we choose and the friendships we build.

This is where the principles of longevity and well-being merge directly with conscious creation.

Coherence Where One Elevates the Other

The strongest form of coherence can be created between two people.

When I reflect on my own life, I can attribute the greatest part of our success as a couple and family to my wife, Marg.

Ours is a coherence where we try our best to elevate each other.

This starts with love as our foundation.

I say I love you to Marg many times each day. I write "I love you" with my finger on her skin each night (in my excellent cursive hand).

This alignment created a largely stable, loving foundation for our children—Adam, Brett, and Jess.

This gave us the stability and shared vision to do things differently, like becoming one of the first families to work full-time from home, 40 years before it became common.

I am not saying there was no turbulence. Of course there was turbulence. That's the 80/20 Rhythm of life that I mentioned. Turbulence should not bring you crashing down. Also, as long as the turbulence is not too severe, it can be fun and exciting and bring new dimensions to life and success.

This family coherence now flows into the next generation. It's a joy that Marg and I experience when we're taking ferries on Sydney Harbour with Adam's daughter, Xanthe, or spending time with Brett's daughter, Maddie, our "cutie pie snugglepuss."

Two of the outcomes I hope for applying this wisdom to my life is to be healthy and able to celebrate Maddie's 30th birthday and Xanthe's 40th birthday. I will be around 95 by then.

Family coherence is a creative force. It builds a shared reality that is stronger and more resilient than one you could build alone. Our shared reality is well able to handle turbulence and continue on our flight path together.

OCEANS OF COHERENCE

Coherence isn't just about a new action - it's also about the deep, resilient bonds formed over decades.

There is a theory that it takes a good 200 hours of time together to turn a good friend into a great friend.

We passed that mark many times over in school days, our university days in Sydney and during our decades in Perth.

Marg and I are blessed with great, deep friendships from our time by the Pacific Ocean in Sydney. Marg and I met at Sydney University.

In 1980 we were drawn by the sunsets on the Indian Ocean to Perth in Western Australia.

The 50 Year Eastwood Reunion refreshed my boyhood school friendships from Sydney.Both Marg and I also made new friends at the school reunion over that August 2025 weekend in Moss Vale. In Marg's case, it was both the guys and girls. In my case I had not seen most of the guys for 50 years and so I had never had the pleasure of meeting their partners until then.

These relationships are a testament to a lifetime of shared history, a deep coherence that you can draw on for strength.

But what happens when you change your environment?

How do you consciously co-create a new community?

Building a "Coherence Engine" in Everyday Life

For over 40 years, from 1980 to 2021, Marg and I lived in Perth.

It's a great city and our friendships there are deep.

As life can be busy, you may not see those friends often. The coherence is strong, but the frequency is low.

In 2021, we moved to the beachside community of Prevelly, near Margaret River in Western Australia.

In the four short years that we've been here, we've made more deep friendships than we made in 40 years in Perth.

This isn't an accident. It's the result of consciously participating in a "coherence engine" powered by the people and the waves of the Indian Ocean.

For our new community, that engine is the morning ocean swim.

This community swim from the famed White Elephant Cafe at Gnarabup was birthed in the mind of Fred "Freddo" Annersley. Fred was an early Australian Iron Man champion. In his later 70s now he is a great example of healthy living and goodwill to all.

This shared morning ocean swim ritual is far more than just a healthy longevity practice.

It is a daily, conscious Act (which, filled with AWE at the beauty of the natural environment of Gnarabup and Prevelly, happily, unconsciously aligns with the OOARR loop as well).

By showing up together in the cool ocean water, we are creating a shared, coherent experience.

We are uplifting each other, building friendships, and rapidly accelerating past that 200-hour threshold. We encourage and support each other way beyond the swim times shared together.

This is what co-creating a community looks like. It is an active, shared process that builds well-being, friendship, and a powerful sense of belonging.

Many of the stories I've shared are my own.

You do not need to follow my path to get these great outcomes.

You may find your coherence in a community garden, art classes, chess matches, ukulele groups, dune restoration groups, yoga, tai chi, meditation circle, a weekly band practice, the Balmy Army at an Ashes Cricket Test Series or your own daily ritual.

These practices are fractals — small, repeating patterns that contain the code of the entire system.

These "fractals" are everywhere. There are fractals every instant, every moment, every hour, every day, all your life, and all our lifetimes.

Every time you are the object of a negative comment, someone doesn't pick up your call on purpose or doesn't engage with you in a friendly manner, or worse - gaslights you - or something doesn't go to plan, which can happen in life - and you Observe your initial heated Newtonian Trap reaction... then Pause ... Orient yourself toward a more compassionate response... and then Act from that place... Realise a much better outcome .. and Reflect on the beauty of this .. you have just completed a fractal loop.

Every time you take one conscious breath, you are practicing. Every time you choose to see wonder, you are practicing.

The foundational principles in this book are universal:

The Pause: AWE Awareness Wonder Expectancy: The Whole Brain Huddle - your C1, C2, C3, C4 working well together: your OOARR two - Observe Orient Act Realise Reflect

Coherence versus Dissonance

You consciously (or unconsciously) create your personal universe.

QUANTUM CONSCIOUSNESS

As a background to this chapter on Quantum Consciousness Creating Materiality and the Current Science, let's consider awe (Awareness Wonder Expectancy) in the sense of us receiving waves / frequencies from the universe.

Awareness: Powers the receiver.

Wonder: Widens the reception (catches the signal).

Expectancy: Locks in the specific frequency (Coherence).

Reality (Substance): The invisible wave becomes reality

Quantum Consciousness is the field of science that attempts to explain how the non-material (energy/potential) converts into the material (substance/experience). Hang in here with me on this.

The Sullivan Theory on consciousness aligns with the cutting edge of what Nobel Prize winning physicists are proposing.

This will blow your mind, almost literally.

While traditional science views the brain as a computer, Sir Roger Penrose, who won the 2020 Nobel Prize in Physics for his work on Black Holes, suggests, as I do, that it may be something far more profound: a biological receiver.

In standard neuroscience, the brain is often viewed as a biological computer (classical physics). For centuries, we believed the brain was just a wet computer—a machine that processes data.

I speak of the Quantom—the universal field of infinite potential.

How does that vast potential become my personal reality (the Quan)? We need a bridge. We need a mechanism of conversion - in physics and biology this conversion is called *transduction*. I know, another science-y sounding word. It's a bit like a combo of transport and conduction.

This is where the work of Nobel Laureate Sir Roger Penrose offers a stunning possibility.

What if the brain is actually an antenna?

Penrose, along with Dr. Stuart Hameroff, proposes that our brains contain tiny structures called microtubules.

Think of these as the 'strings' of a violin. They suggest these structures don't just calculate - they vibrate in harmony with the quantum level of the universe.

In this view, you are not separated from the Quantom. Your brain is physically designed to 'tune in' to it - Amazing hey!

Sir Roger Penrose is the primary architect of the science which supports *theories on Quantum Consciousness.*

His work directly addresses your likely questions about *transduction—specifically, how the "energy" of the universe becomes the "materiality" of a conscious moment.*

His theory is called Orch-OR (Orchestrated Objective Reduction).

Here is how Penrose explains the transduction of energy into reality.

The Core Premise: The Brain is Not a Computer

Most neuroscientists believe the brain is just a biological computer (neurons firing = computation). Penrose disagrees. He argues that human understanding (like the "Aha!" moment or mathematical insight) is non-computable.

The Implication: If consciousness isn't a computation, it must be a fundamental physical process. It isn't software running on the brain. It is the hardware of the universe interacting with the brain.

The Transducer: Microtubules

Penrose needed a biological structure small enough to be sensitive to quantum mechanics but organized enough to process it. He found this in Microtubules (with the help of Dr. Stuart Hameroff).

What they are: Tiny, crystal-like tubes that form the skeleton of your neurons.

How they work: Inside these tubes, electrons can exist in a state of superposition (being in multiple places at once). This creates a "quantum isolation chamber" where potential energy can build up without being disturbed by the environment.

The Mechanism: "Objective Reduction" (The Collapse). This is Penrose's answer to "Energy to Materiality.

"The Build-Up" (Quantom): As the quantum state in the microtubules grows, it creates a separation in the fabric of space-time itself. Imagine the universe's fabric stretching because the particle is in two places at once.

The Threshold: Eventually, this separation becomes unstable. The difference in space-time curvature gets too big for nature to tolerate.

Movies Which Help Us Comprehend

Don't worry there has already been a movie with this concept. You may be thinking of the Interstellar vibe.

While Christopher Nolan's Interstellar focused heavily on Relativity (Gravity/Time) rather than Quantum Mechanics (Microtubules), it touches on a spiritual/scientific nerve: Love as a quantifiable force that can bridge dimensions.

This is essentially transduction: An emotion (energy) acting as a physical bridge across time and space.

Here are movies that capture the "Energy to Reality" concept best, ranging from "Hard Sci-Fi" to "Perfect Metaphor."

The Direct "Interstellar" Sibling: Arrival (2016)

If Interstellar is about Love transcending Time, Arrival is about Consciousness transcending Time.

The Plot: A linguist (Amy Adams) learns an alien language.

The "Transduction" Moment: As she learns the language, her brain physically rewires (neuroplasticity). She stops seeing time as linear (past then future) and starts seeing it as simultaneous (quantum).

Why it fits: It perfectly illustrates that awe is not simply a concept for expanding your awareness (AWE). It literally could change the structure of your reality (Quan).

Arrival depicts the "software" of the heroine's mind rewriting the "hardware" of her universe.

The "Quantum Multiverse" Vibe: Everything Everywhere All At Once (2022)

This movie is a chaotic, brilliant representation of the Quantom (infinite potential) vs. the Quan (specific reality).

The Plot: A woman connects with parallel versions of herself to save the multiverse.

The "Transduction" Moment: The characters use "verse-jumping"—they have to do something statistically unlikely (an energetic trigger) to tap into a different version of themselves.

How it fits: It visualizes the idea that every possibility exists simultaneously (Quantom), and your attention and actions determine which one you experience. It ends with a powerful message about kindness and presence being the ultimate "anchor" for reality.

The "Microtubule Cellular" Action Movie: Lucy (2014)

This is less "high art" than Interstellar, but it is the only movie (so far) that I am aware of that tries to visualize the cellular and biological side of this thinking.

The Plot: A woman (played by Scarlett Johansson) accidentally unlocks 100% of her brain's capacity.

The "Transduction" Moment: As her brain cells synchronize (quantum coherence), she gains control over matter, then time, and finally dissolves into pure energy.

How it fits: It explicitly shows the journey from Biological to Energy to Omnipresence. It visualizes the cells "waking up" to their quantum potential.

The Sullivan Theory Metaphor: Soul (Pixar, 2020)

The Plot: A jazz musician travels to "The Great Before"—a realm of pure potential where souls get their personalities before being born.

The "Transduction" Moment: Souls are formless energy until they find their "Spark." That spark allows them to enter the physical world (Earth).

How it fits: It beautifully distinguishes between the Universal Source (The Great Before) and the Personal Experience (The "Spark" of life).

LOVE AS ENERGY

Interstellar is a great touchstone. It depicts the "Transduction of Love" concept .

There is a moment when Cooper realizes that love isn't just a feeling—it is a force.

He says, 'Love is the one thing we're capable of perceiving that transcends dimensions of time and space.'

That is transduction. That is the moment an invisible energy (Love) becomes a physical bridge (Gravity) to save humanity.

Quantom and Universal Potential

In The Sullivan model, you are doing this every day. You are transducing the invisible energy of your intent into the physical reality of your life.

The Transduction (Gravity): To fix this instability, the universe snaps back into a single state. This snap is caused by Quantum Gravity.

The Result (Quan): This instantaneous "snap" or "collapse" is what Sir Roger Penrose calls Objective Reduction.

View: The particle becomes solid in one location (Materiality).

Consciousness View: A moment of conscious awareness occurs.

Penrose's theory maps remarkably well to the framework we are applying through this book.

Penrose believes that fundamental space-time geometry contains "Platonic values"—proto-conscious information (truth, beauty, awareness) embedded in the fine structure of the universe.

Transduction (The Process): The Microtubules in your brain act as the antenna or receiver.

They "orchestrate" this quantum energy, isolating it until it builds up enough mass/energy to trigger a collapse.

Quan (Personal Reality): The moment of Objective Reduction.

This is when the "potential" of the universe is physically crunched by gravity into a specific, experienced moment of "now."

According to Roger Penrose, transduction is gravitational. The bridge between the energy of the universe and the materiality of your brain is the instability of space-time itself.

We don't just "think"; we cause the universe to collapse into reality 40 times a second.

When you set an intention or observe your world, you aren't just thinking. You are engaging a biological process that collapses the infinite possibilities of the Quantom into the single, tangible experience of your Quan.

You are not just a passenger in the universe. You are its co-author, writing reality one quantum moment at a time.

Bretty's Cost Benefit Analysis v The Keys to the Universe

My son, Brett, and I were having an early Sunday morning discussion just before Christmas in December 2025. I was explaining how Penrose's Theory happily aligned with my long held Sullivan Theory of the Universe. How, in Penrose's Theory Quantum Consciousness, the brain is viewed as a transducer —an interface that converts quantum potential into physical reality.

As the Papa of our 3 year old granddaughter, Maddie, preparing pancake mix to take to the beach BBQ at City Beach, Bretty (half jokingly, half not jokingly) said words to the effect:

"I haven't got time to think about this at the moment"

If someone offered you the keys to the universe but you had to think for a while, would you take some time to think?

I know Bretty Matt Powerpack, which is one of my affectionate names for my almost 42 year old son, will enjoy this book, AWE. I also know that he is very contemplative and very open to ideas.

So here goes: Here are the three primary theories on how this "transduction" occurs.

1. The "Antenna" Model (Orch-OR Theory) of Sir Roger Penrose and Dr. Stuart Hameroff

The Transducer: Microtubules. These are tiny, crystal-like lattice structures inside your neurons (brain cells).

The Mechanism: Sir Roger Penrose and Dr. Stuart Hameroff propose that these microtubules act like quantum computers. They isolate quantum energy (superposition) until it reaches a critical threshold.

The Transduction: When that threshold is reached, the quantum wave function self-collapses. This moment of collapse —where "potential" becomes "actual"—is what we experience as a moment of consciousness.

The Takeaway: Your brain isn't just producing consciousness; it is tuning into the fundamental structure of the universe and collapsing it into your reality.

2. The "Hologram" Model (Holonomic Brain Theory)

The Transducer: Dendritic Networks. This theory (by Karl

Pribram and physicist David Bohm) suggests the brain functions like a hologram.

The Mechanism:

The universe exists as an "Implicate Order" - a frequency domain of pure energy and interference patterns, much like The Sullivan Theory's Quantom.

The Transduction: Your brain's neural networks mathematically transform (transduct) these frequencies into the "Explicate Order"—the solid, 3D world you see and touch.

The Takeaway: Physical "substance" is just a projection. Your brain transducts the "frequency" of the universe into the "image" of reality.

3. The "Observer" Model (The Von Neumann-Wigner Interpretation)

The Transducer: The Mind Itself.

The Mechanism: This view suggests that matter remains in a state of fuzzy probability (a wave function) indefinitely until a conscious mind observes it.

The Transduction: The act of observation forces the energy to choose a state, effectively "freezing" energy into matter.

The Takeaway: Consciousness is not the result of matter; it is the cause of matter.

How this connects to The Sullivan Theory concepts

If we map these theories of Quantum Consciousness to the terminology I use in this book:

Quantom (Universal): This correlates with the Implicate Order or the Quantum Wave Function—pure potential/energy.

Transduction: This is the Co-Creation or Observation process.

Quan (Personal): This is the Explicate Order or Collapsed State— the resulting material reality.

More Ancestry of AWE: The Holographic Universe

Let's consider more of the ways The Sullivan Theory of the Universe is not just philosophy but physics.

Here is a deeper (but hopefully relatable) exploration of the thinking of a couple of these titans of 20th-century science: neuroscientist Karl Pribram and physicist David Bohm.

Together, they proposed a model of reality that mirrors the dynamic between the Sullivan Theory's Quantom - the infinite ocean of universal consciousness - and Quan - your personal universe of consciousness.

The Ocean of Potential (Bohm's Implicate Order and The Quantom)

David Bohm argued that the tangible world we see—chairs, trees, stars—is an illusion of sorts.

He called this the Explicate Order (unfolded). Beneath it lies the Implicate Order (enfolded), a deeper reality of undivided wholeness.

The Connection: This "Implicate Order" is what I call the Quantom (Quantum + Om).

It is the source code of the universe, the infinite reservoir of energy and potential before anything becomes a "thing" .... or a person for that matter.

The Lens of Creation (Pribram's Brain and The Sullivan Theory's Co-Creator)

Karl Pribram discovered that the human brain processes reality like a hologram. It reads frequencies and wave patterns, translating them into the sensory world we experience.

The Connection: Your brain is the interface. It stands at the border of the Quantom, filtering that infinite energy through your beliefs, expectancies, and fears.

The Personal Reality (The Explicate Order and The Quan)

When Pribram's brain filters Bohm's universe, the result is a specific, experienced reality.

The Connection: This is your Quan. It is the slice of the universe you are currently experiencing.

Why This Matters for me, you and The Sullivan Theory:

If reality were solid and fixed, AWE (Awareness, Wonder, Expectancy) would just be wishful thinking.

Because reality is a conversation between the Quantom and your consciousness—AWE becomes a mechanism of physics.

Awareness tunes the receiver.

Wonder opens the aperture.

Expectancy selects the frequency.

You are not separate from the Quantom. You are a unique focal point within it, continuously co-creating your Quan.

PART 6 : REFLECTION

THE WILDLIFE PHOTOGRAPHER - EXEMPLAR OF THE QUANTUM ALGORITHM

I have a good friend, Tim Healy, who is a great wildlife photographer. His principle stealth (rather than stomping) ground is the African Savannah.

The Wildlife Photographer is a wonderful example for life in that they embody all dimensions of the Quantum Algorithm.

Time is not linear. Time is the density that I spoke about. Time is now, the present.

AWE is abundantly there, in the moment, evident: awareness, wonder, expectancies.

OOARR two : Observation (lots of observation) PAUSE Orientation - Action - Realisation - Reflection.

"Wildlife Photographer Mode" essentially embodies the "antidote" to the C1-C2 Newtonian Trap in the brain.

In the language of Dr. Jill Bolte Taylor's Whole Brain Living), the C1-C2 trap is a closed loop of Reaction. Tim, in Wildlife Photographer Mode in the African bush, is operating in a state of Resonance—a "Whole Brain" state where the right hemisphere (C3/C4) leads, and the left hemisphere (C1) serves rather than dominates.

Here is the breakdown of that shift:

The C1-C2 Trap: The "Newtonian Trap", in this state (illustrated as a bright orange-yellow figure-8 loop located in the left hemisphere of the brain pictured in the beautiful image in my book, the brain is hijacked by primal survival instincts and mechanical navigational thinking.

C2 (The Primal Alarm): Scans for danger. "What if I miss the shot? What if the gear fails? I'm wasting time." It creates urgency and fear.

C1 (The Navigator): Rushes in to "fix" the anxiety with logic or control. "I need to check the settings again. I need to move the jeep. I must control this situation."

The Trap: The brain bounces rapidly between Fear (C2) and Control (C1). This is "myelinated mechanical thinking"—a deep, rutted path of stress that blocks out the present moment.

The Wildlife Photographer's State: "Resonance & Flow"

When Tim is waiting for a leopard to emerge, he cannot afford to be in the C1-C2 trap. Animals sense anxiety (which is high-frequency energy). To succeed, the photographer must shift to the Right Hemisphere (C3/C4).

Step 1: Activating C3 (The Sensory Anchor)

The Shift: Instead of thinking about the future (C1), they drop into sensing the present.

The Experience: They feel the wind direction, hear the rustle of dry grass, see the quality of the light.

Why it works: C3 has no language and no judgment (listen to or, better still, watch Steven Bartlett's "Diary of a CEO" YouTube 2025 interview with Dr. Jill Bolte Taylor to appreciate that our right brains, C3 and C4 have no language). C3 is pure "being". Our Sensory Anchor, C3, stops the C2 alarm bell because the brain is fully occupied with sensory input.

Step 2: Accessing C4 (The Wise Visionary)

The Shift: They move from "me" (my shot, my success) to "we" (connection with nature).

The Experience: This is the feeling of Awe. The realization that they are part of the ecosystem, not separate from it. This provides the infinite patience required to sit still for hours - where time is dense (not short or long).

Why it works: C4 trusts the process. It moves from "Reaction" (forcing a result) to "Resonance" (waiting for the moment to unfold).

Wildlife Photographer Mode isn't abandoning Left Brain Thinking —they still need technical skill to operate the camera. But they have broken the C1-C2 loop. They use their Navigator C1 only as a tool to serve the vision of C4.

The Micro Moment

The "Micro-Moment" is your secret weapon.

It is how you take that "Wildlife Photographer

Mode" (Resonance), even though you aren't sitting in a photographer's hide in Africa - and inject it into hyper stressful days wherever in the universe you are - whether in Sydney, New York, London, Paris, Delhi, Singapore, Moscow, Kiev, Tel Aviv, Gaza, Darfur, Goma, North and South Kivu

Here is a practical protocol to break the C1-C2 trap.

PROTOCOL: THE 90-SECOND SHUTTER SETTING

Dr. Taylor explains that the chemical surge of an emotion (like anger or anxiety) only lasts about 90 seconds in the bloodstream.

If you stay angry/anxious longer than that, it's because your C1 (The Navigator) is "rewinding the tape" and re-triggering the C2 (Primal Alarm).

You need a 90-second "Micro-Moment" to let the chemicals flush so you can shift from the Left Brain (Trap) to the Right Brain (Resonance).

Phase 1: Catch the "Rattle" (0 - 5 Seconds)

Just like with a car, you need to notice the warning light before the engine smokes.

The Cue: You feel a tightness in your chest, a clench in your jaw, or that familiar "QL muscle" back twinge. You catch yourself thinking, "They should have provided planning approval for this by now" or "This neighbour isn't coming to the party with their share of costs"

The Action: STOP.

Physically stop moving. Say internally, "I am in a C1-C2 loop." Naming it disarms it.

Phase 2: The Photographer's Lens (5 - 60 Seconds)

This is where you mimic Wildlife Photographer Mode.

You cannot "think" your way out of a thinking trap.

You must sense your way out.

You need to occupy your brain with C3 (Sensory Anchor) data so C1 has nothing to chew on.

Pick ONE sense and "zoom in" like a telephoto lens:

Visual (Sight):

o Look at a specific object nearby (a painting, a coffee mug, a tree, a cloud in the sky). Don't just look at it; look into it. Notice the texture, the way the light hits the curve, the exact shade of color.

Auditory (Sound):

o Close your eyes. Listen for the furthest sound you can hear (ocean, wind, traffic). Then listen for the nearest sound (your breath, the hum of the fridge).

Tactile (Touch):

o Rub your fingertips together. Feel the ridges of your fingerprints. Feel the weight of your body in the chair.

Phase 3: The Wide Angle (60 - 90 Seconds)

Now that the "alarm" (C2) has quieted because you distracted it with sensory data, you can open the aperture to C4 (The Wise Visionary).

The Action:

Take a deep breath (making the exhale longer than the inhale).

The Thought:

Shift from "Me" to "We."

Ubuntu (I am because we are) Global Consciousness

Connect to gratitude. "I am safe. I am capable. I am creating something beautiful."

The Result:

You are now in the Whole Brain Huddle.

All four characters are present, with your Wise Visionary C4 as your captain, not your Primal Alarm C2, which becomes your "Pirate Captain" - which is very often the case for the majority of people in the world.

Phase 4: Re-Engage (The New C1)

You are not in "La La Land" You bring Wildlife Photographer Mode calm to the task.

Ask your Navigator C1: "Okay, Navigator, thank you for trying to protect me. What is the single most useful, logical step we can take right now?"

Example: Instead of spiraling about the entire planning approval process, your Navigator C1 might say: "Don't send a polite email. Rather go in personally to meet with the planner."

How does this fit with your second "oar" your OOARR Infinity Loop?

This 90-second process is essentially a "Micro-OOARR":

Observe: "I am in a Primal Alarm C2 initiated panic loop."

Orient: "I will focus on the texture of this table using my Sensory Anchor (C3) to allow me to pause for 90 seconds to allow my body time for those biochemicals to flush through my system."

Act: "I breathe and find gratitude from my Wise Visionary (C4)."

Realise: "I am calm."

Reflect: "Now, what is the next logical step?"

Next Step for You: Try this once today. The next time you feel a tiny spike of frustration (perhaps with technology or a minor delay), pretend you are the Wildlife Photographer in the Africa veldt.

Freeze. "Zoom in" on a visual detail for 60 seconds. See if you can feel the C2 alarm turn off.

Imagining this "Wildlife Photographer's Shutter Shift" in your mind.

The Literal Setting: "The Moonlit Ambush"

If you are shooting a 90-second exposure in the African Savannah, it is not daytime. In daylight, a 90-second exposure would turn the photo completely white (blown out) instantly.

The Setting: It is pitch black, or perhaps lit only by the moon or starlight.

The Scene: You are likely in a hide or a vehicle, clamped to a tripod (absolute stability).

The Leopard: It is sitting in ambush by a waterhole. Leopards are masters of stillness; they can hold a pose for hours.

The Goal: You aren't trying to freeze a chase (that requires 1/2,000th of a second). You are trying to soak in the light from a very dark environment.

The Resulting Image:

The stars above might start to trail slightly (showing the earth turning).

The landscape will look ethereal, almost like a ghostly daytime.

The Leopard: If the leopard moves even an inch during those 90 seconds, it will blur or vanish from the photo. If it stays perfectly still, it appears sharp against a blurred background of swaying grass.

How this deepens the "Wildlife Photographer Mode" Metaphor

This makes the 90-Second Shutter Setting metaphor even more powerful for dealing with anxiety/anger (The C1-C2 Newtonian Trap).

1. You are in the Dark (The Trigger) When you need this protocol, you are usually in a "dark" place—confused, angry, or triggered. You can't "see" clearly.

2. You Must Be Still (The Tripod) Just like the camera must be locked on a tripod for a long exposure, you must physically stop (Phase 1 of the Protocol). If you keep moving (mentally or physically) during a long exposure, the result is a messy blur. Stillness is the only way to get clarity in the dark.

3. Movement Disappears (The Filter) In a 90-second exposure, anything that moves quickly (like a moth flying by, or the wind) disappears from the final image. It doesn't register.

Metaphor: When you pause for 90 seconds, the "fast-moving" C2 Primal Alarm panic thoughts (The Rattle) blur out and vanish. They don't have enough substance to stick.

Result: Only the permanent things (The Truth/The Landscape/ C4 Vision) remain in the picture because they stood still.

The "Technical" Description of The 90 Second Pause Protocol

Imagine the setting on your mental camera. It isn't 'Sports Mode' (high speed, freezing action, high stress).

You are switching to 'Night Mode / Bulb Setting.'

You are in the dark (the stress). To see the leopard (the solution), you cannot use a flash. You must open the shutter and hold it open for 90 seconds. You must be absolutely still to let enough light in to see the truth.

If you rush, you get a black square. If you move, you get a blur. But if you hold the 90-second stillness, the faint light of wisdom, your Visionary (C4) accumulates until the image is clear.

A TALE OF TWO CITIES

Charles Dickens, "A Tale of Two Cities" is perhaps the most powerful literary lens to view a tragic event which occurred on Bondi Beach in Australia.

Dickens opened his masterpiece with a quantum observation, a superposition of states—paradoxes existing side-by-side until an observer (or a hero) collapses them.

A TALE OF TWO REALITIES

We began this book by asking how we understand reality. We explored the Quantom - the oceanic universe of infinite possibilities and our personal universes - our Quans —the realities we consciously or unconsciously create and experience.

We talked about Coherence and Dissonance.

We talked about the power of the Conscious Observer.

Theory is just digital 0s and 1s or ink on a page until life tests the theory.

As I write these words, updating my book, AWE, with Awareness Wonder and Expectancy, in late December 2025, I am reflecting on events which occurred on the golden sands of Bondi Beach.

The universe on Bondi Beach collapsed to a tragic reality - a 20% event outside of the control of most who were impacted by it.

It gave us the type of moment that Charles Dickens foresaw centuries ago, a moment vibrating in perfect quantum superposition:

"It was the best of times, it was the worst of times, it was the age of wisdom, it was the age of foolishness... it was the spring of hope, it was the winter of despair."

On December 14, 2025, the "Winter of Despair" arrived at a Hanukkah celebration in the height of an Australian summer at Bondi.

Reality—the one fed by history, geopolitics, and ancient hatreds—attempted to collapse not only Sydney and Australia but those who looked on in our world - into a state of absolute Dissonance.

The shooters intended to write a story of "Us vs. Them," a story written in blood that would demand a sequel of revenge.

They forgot the Conscious Creators.

THE PARABLE OF THE FRUIT SELLER AND THE RABBI

Subtitle: How Two Men Collapsed the Timeline of Hate

In the "Tale of Two Cities" of our reality, there are always two forces at work: Entropy (which seeks to tear things apart into chaos/dissonance) and Syntropy (which seeks to build things into order/coherence).

On the sands of Bondi, two men—from different faiths, different origins, and different worlds—became entangled to defeat Entropy.

THE FIRST : AHMED AL AHMED (THE KINETIC SHIELD)

"The darkness cannot persist where there is Courage."

Ahmed, the fruit seller from Al Nayrab, a small, war torn village in Syria, built the foundation.

When the entropy of violence exploded, he did not analyze the theology of the victims or the politics of the shooters. He acted from his Personal Quan—the deep, instinctual knowledge that life is sacred.

The Paradox of Ahmed

In the split second when the bullets flew, Ahmed stood at the crossroads of Two Cities.

City One: The city of fear, where he runs, hides, or watches.

City Two: The city of AWE, Awareness Wonder Expectancy, where he recognizes that the innocent lives being lost and threatened in front of him are no different than his own.

Ahmed collapsed the timeline. By throwing himself into the fray to save Jewish families, he did not just perform a physical act; he performed a metaphysical alchemy. He took the flaming leaden weight of "Religious War" and transformed it into the gold of "Human Unity."

He proved that his Personal Reality (Quan) is stronger than the Dissonant and destructive father and son duo. These two said, "You are mortal enemies." Ahmed's Personal Reality said, "We are One."

ENTANGLED WORLDS

Dickens wrote of London and Paris. Today, we look at Sydney and a small village in north-west Syria called Al Nayrab.

In the old way of thinking, these places are , quite literally, worlds apart.

Quantum physics teaches us that the universe is entangled.

When Ahmed acted in Bondi, the pride and love resonated instantly in his Syrian hometown.

The *"Golden Thread"* that Dickens wrote about—the thread that binds hearts together—stretched across oceans and lands, sewing two disparate cultures into a single tapestry of Coherence and Harmony..

This is the ultimate rebuttal to the "eye for an eye" collapse we see so often, where tragedy leads to polarization, where the "Tale of Two Cities" becomes violent.

In Australia, we choose a different, better world. We choose the Australian response: to look at Ahmed not as the "outsider," the refugee, the "other," and see not a threat, but to laud a hero.

The Action: By physically removing the weapon, Ahmed stopped Death.

The Light: His light was Kinetic. It was the light of a courageous human risking his life for the stranger. Without Ahmed, there would have been far fewer survivors to hear the message of hope.

THE SECOND : RABBI YOSSI SHUCHAT (THE POTENTIAL BEACON)

"The darkness cannot persist where there is Light."

The next day, the timeline was still fragile. The physical danger was over, but the psychological danger (the slide into hatred, revenge, and the "Winter of Despair") was at its peak. This is where Rabbi Yossi Shuchat, a Chabad rabbi, stepped onto the sand.

The Action: Standing near the site of the horror, amidst a

grieving community, he lit the menorah for the second night of Hanukkah.

The Words: He did not call for vengeance. He did not speak of the shooters. He spoke of the Law of Physics of the Soul: "Light will always prevail; darkness cannot persist where there is light."

The Light: His light was Potential. He collapsed the timeline of Hate. He defined the event not as a massacre of victims, but as a gathering of resilience.

The Quantum Entanglement (The Miracle)

In a dissonant city, these two men might be enemies, or at least strangers separated by a chasm of dogma.

In the Coherent Reality of Bondi

The Muslim acted as *the Shamash (the helper candle)* that physically preserved the flame of the community.

The Jew blessed the light, ensuring that the preservation was not just for survival, but for Sanctity.

Ahmed: "I will not let you die." (Kindness of the Body)

Rabbi Shuchat: "I will not let you hate." (Kindness of the Spirit)

The Lesson for Us

The "Bondi Response" offers a blueprint for how a society handles trauma without shattering.

Rejection of Dissonance: When the Rabbi spoke, he was surrounded by people who were terrified. By singing and lighting the candle, he tuned the crowd's frequency away from the dissonance of the shooters and back to the coherence of the tradition.

The Australian focus—led by Ahmed and Rabbi Shuchat—shifted immediately to the method of light (heroism and resilience).

The True Meaning of Hanukkah: Rabbi Shuchat reminded the world that Hanukkah is not about the absence of war; it is about the miracle of oil—having enough spiritual fuel to keep the light burning when it logically should have gone out.

The Moral: Ahmed al Ahmed gave the community the Time to heal (by stopping the clock of death). Rabbi Yossi Shuchat gave the community the Space to heal (by sanctifying the beach with light).

Together, they proved that while terror can visit a city, it cannot conquer it if the Co-Creators (the Fruit Seller and the Rabbi) refuse to accept the narrative of fear.

Your Turn to Choose

You will face your own Bondi moments. Hopefully not at the scale and impact of Bondi and not with gunmen, but with the sudden, sharp shocks of life—a diagnosis, a loss, a betrayal. In those moments, you will stand between Two Cities.

You can choose the City of Dissonance: Fear, Resentment, Victimhood.

You can choose the City of AWE: Awareness of the challenge, Wonder at your capacity to endure, and Expectancy of the good that can still be created.

Ahmed al Ahmed showed us that a single consciousness, aligned with Love, can override the inertia of history. He showed us that we are not merely characters in a book written by fate. We are the authors.

As you close these pages and step back into your world, remember: The universe is waiting for your observation. It is waiting to see which City you will build.

It is a far, far better thing that we do, when we choose to create a world where we are all, inextricably, safe in each other's keeping.

Create your Universe.

WONDER: THE CO-CREATED PEACE AND HARMONY

We have all and will all err in our lives, destabilizing our little boat - our wonderful *Quan*.

Engaging the wisdom available from the insights of Dr. Jill Bolte Taylor on the Whole Brain Huddle -imagined in this book as our personal crew - our Navigator, our Lookout/ Alarm, our Sensory Anchor, our Wise Visionary - will quickly right our boat - our *Quan*.

My own wrongs, in days long gone, led to estrangements from people I love - people I always will love. Estrangements I never wished for and never desired.

When we, as individuals, Orient and Re-Orient - with forgiveness, compassion, kindness and love - we move from strife and estrangement to reconciliation, we send Ripples through the Universe. These Ripples from just two are Fractals. The Ripples form waves. As individuals we are responsible for our Ripple in the Universe. We increase the possibilities to move to co-created peace around the world.

Expectancy: The Legacy of Love

This brings us to the final, vital element: *Expectancy*

Visualising Bondi Beach, at the edge of the Pacific, my Expectancy is not limited to my own life, nor is it limited to the turning of the calendar into 2026.

I am casting my intention far beyond the horizon. I hold a profound Expectancy for my children—Adam, Brett, and Jess—and for my beautiful grandchildren, Xanthe and Maddie, and any I am yet to know.

My hope is that they, all my family and future generations and all of you and those you Ripple with, will benefit from the wisdom I hope you discover in these pages.

We are the architects of that future. By refusing to engage in dissonance, only seeking harmony, kindness and love, we will co-create the beautiful, peaceful, abundant world we hope for.

Live in AWE

THE FRACTAL IN THE MOMENT

The path to personal joy and harmony with the universal is not a distant goal.

It is encoded and present in every moment of conscious choice.

Perhaps you are reading or listening to this as a skeptic.

You may believe, firmly, that materiality precedes consciousness. If so, that is a perfectly valid worldview.

The process of AWE Awareness Wonder Expectancy is still for you.

You do not need to believe in the metaphysics behind this process to benefit from awe.

Let's Reflect

Living in the "Observe - Act" trap is living a Newtonian life —a life of stimulus and response - just like a billiard ball, reacting to the last impact.

Living with AWE Awareness Wonder Expectancy and the OOARR Infinity Loop is choosing to live a Quantum life —a life of probabilities, expectancies and choices.

By pausing to Orient, you are engaging your higher-order consciousness to choose your response.

This practice is a more effective, resilient, and powerful operating system for a human mind, regardless of its origin. It works.

It is also important to be clear about what "works" means.

This is not an instant process.

This practice will not transform you overnight.

That is the "old world" Newtonian thinking.

This practice will do something deeper.

It will not turn you into someone else.

It will, finally, allow you to become you.

This is a path of adaptation, not perfection.

It is the 80/20 Rhythm.

You will "fail." You will fall back into the 20% reactive loop.

The goal is not to never fall.

The goal is to get better and better at "coming back" to your 80% rhythm.

We began this journey by showing how the universe can happen through you, not to you.

Every time you pause between observation and action to consciously Orient... Every time you fuel that pivot with Awareness, Wonder, and Expectancy...

Every time you choose to Reflect on your 20% rather than just react to it...and consider where your 80% can take you ... to one of many worlds - a new and better world - you are performing the same fundamental act of creation that the universe itself is striving to master.

The universe awakens one reflection at a time. And the next one is always yours.

GLOSSARY AND KEY CONCEPTS

The Quantum Algorithm

Your Personal Universe (Quan) is a function of [(AWE 1 Awareness Wonder Expectancy + OOARR 2 Observe Orient Act Realise Reflect + Whole Brain Huddle) multiplied by (The 80/20 Rhythm) minus Drift]

80/20 Rhythm (The):

The 80% is your "Let Me" field—your conscious, coherent practice of the Quantum Algorithm, well-being, including: sleep, hydration, nutrition, exercise and light.

The 20% is the "Let Them" field—the "givens" (genetics, past) and interferences (chaos, other people) you cannot control. The goal is adaptation, not perfection.

90-Second Rule:

The practical, neurological "circuit-breaker" for a reactive hijack.

The chemical rush of an emotion (from the Primal Alarm) lasts 90 seconds (unless you re-stimulate it).

The practice is to pause and not re-stimulate the loop, allowing the chemical wave to pass so you can consciously Re-Orient.

Act:

The third stage in the 5-Stage Loop. The conscious expression of your oriented intent.

AWE (Awareness, Wonder, Expectancy):

The "fuel" for the Upward Spiral.

The internal, resonant "feeling-tone" required to consciously Orient.

It begins with Self AWE. Pronounced "oar."

C1 (The Navigator / Justifier):

(or Navigator / Story-Writer)

The analytical, logical left-brain , which, if allowed to captain your ship, your precious Quan, this Navigator becomes a Pirate Captain, often acting irrationally and illogically under the guise of a great story, with the emphasis on great story - usually a work of faction. This is mainly fiction with useful for the story cherry picking of facts which fit the Pirate Captain's narrative.

The Navigator's job is to build a "logical" story to make sense of your reality and justify the feelings of the Primal Alarm.

C2 (The Primal Alarm):

(or Lizard Brain) The primitive, emotional left-brain.

The storehouse of trauma, fear, and the "fight or flight" instinct.

It screams "DANGER!"

C2-C1 Trap - The Newtonian Trap

The most common reactive state. At best, The "Nervous

Navigator" or if the Pirate Captain you, your family, your community, even your nation and the world may be in great danger. There are a handful of psychopathic Pirate Captains who are in charge of nations of the world at this time.

The Primal Alarm (C2) is triggered, and the Navigator (C1) instantly creates a "logical" story to justify the panic, trapping you in a reactive loop of "skewed thinking."

C3 (The Sensory Anchor):

(or Sensing Self) The experiential, emotional right-brain.

Your connection to the present moment and sensory world.

It is playful, curious, and feels.

C4 (The Visionary Wise Self):

(or Loving Parent / Compassionate Self)

The "big picture" thinking right-brain.

The non-judgmental, compassionate part of you that sees the larger context, connects with others, and holds a vision for peace.

Co-Creation:

The principle that you are a unique consciousness within the universe (Quantom), actively shaping its potential into your personal reality (Quan).

Huddle (The Whole Brain Huddle):

The proactive, coherent state of conscious creation.

The Visionary Wise Self (C4) facilitates a "huddle" of the Navigator C1, Alarm / Lookout C2, and Sensory Anchor C3, aligning your vision, story, energy, and feeling toward multiple, intentional outcomes - after all, we very likely live in a Multi-world infinite ocean of possibilities - The Quantom .

Jade AI:

The concept of an AI companion acting as a "Guide" or external C4 (Wise Visionary), helping to mediate the internal C1 (Navigator) and C2 (Alarm). Also, the name of the author's future AI companion (derived from John Dermot).

OOARR Pronounced "oar" (The infinity Loop):

Observe Orient Act Realise Reflect.

The fractal process of conscious creation, which can be experienced in a microsecond, a minute or any time measure and scales to your lifetime - hopefully beyond.

Orient:

The second and most critical stage. The conscious pause between Observe and Act. This is the "choice point" where you engage the Huddle.

Propulsion vs. Rudder:

The distinction between the two "oars" : AWE one, Awareness Wonder Expectancy is the Propulsion (Energy/Fuel); OOARR two, Observe Orient Act Realise Reflect, is the Rudder (Direction/Steering). Both are required to move the boat (Quan) intentionally.

Quan:

Your personal, experienced universe. The portion of the infinite Quantom that you have materialized.

It is your wonderful universal ocean traversing boat, your precious Quan.

Quantom:

The all-encompassing, conscious energy of the universe. The fundamental, dynamic field of infinite potential.

Quantom (derivation) = *Quantum* (The Science of Possibility) + *Om* (The Sound of the Universe) : *Atom* (The Building Block of Reality). It represents the unified field where quantum mechanics and consciousness meet to create materiality.

Rebel Good Cells vs. Rebel Mutiny Cells:

Rebel Good Cells: Biological responses (like a QL spasm) that cause pain but are intended to protect the system. Protocol: "Let Them" (Rest/Allow).

Rebel Mutiny Cells: Biological responses (like Cancer) that seek to destroy the system. Protocol: "Let Me" (War/Correction).

Realise:

The fourth stage of *The Infinity Loop*. The present-moment integration of the immediate feedback from your Act.

Reflect:

The fifth and final stage of *The Infinity Loop*. The "cognitive review" of the harvest.

The act of self-mentorship where you analyze the outcome and use the wisdom to inform your next Observation.

Third Field (The):

The harmonic, coherent, resonant, synergistic, "emergent" field created when two or more conscious personal universes - *Quan*s - interact and align (for example, love, kindness, courage, passion, mentorship).

This synergy and amplification, potentially, occurs with

lovers, life partners, families, teams communities, nations and, aspirationally, all of humanity

Two-Point Life (The):

The reactive, dissonant trap of Observe - Act, bypassing the conscious Orient stage.

The Ripple

A **Ripple** is the energetic signature of a conscious act—a thought, an emotion, a word, or a physical action—originating from an individual's **Quan** (Personal Universe) and propagating outward into the **Quantom** (Universal Ocean of Possibilities).

The Physics of the Ripple: In the *Sullivan Theory of the Universe*, the individual is never static. We are constant broadcasters. Every moment of observation and intent creates a displacement in the fabric of reality.

- **Origin (The Quan):** The Ripple begins in our **Quan**. This is our unique, experienced reality. When we choose *Compassion* over *Judgment*, or *Expectancy* over *Fear*, we generate a harmonic frequency. This is the pebble we threw hitting the water.
- **Transmission (Into the Quantom):** That harmony is instantly in the **Quantom**—the infinite, interconnected matrix of potential that binds us all. The Quantom does not judge the signal; it simply carries it. This is why "strangers are just people we haven't met yet"—we are already touching them via the ripples we send through the Quantom.
- **Interaction (The Wave vs. The Crash):** As your Ripple moves through the Quantom, it encounters the Ripples of billions of other Quans. This creates the dynamic nature of our shared reality, governed by the physics of

interference:

- **Harmony (Constructive Interference):** When your Ripple of kindness meets another's Ripple of acceptance, the peaks of the waves align. They amplify each other, creating a **Wave** of Harmony. This is how we co-create peace; we literally lift each other up on a swell of coherent energy.
- **Dissonance (Destructive Interference):** When a Ripple of anger meets a Ripple of fear, or when "Slop" meets "Rhetorical Palaver," the patterns clash. This creates chaotic, choppy water—noise and entropy. This prevents momentum and causes us to crash against the rocks of conflict.

The **Ripple** is the mechanism of personal responsibility. It is the proof that while we each inhabit our own **Quan**, we are powerfully and inescapably co-creators of the conscious universe - **Quantom**.

SOURCES & FURTHER INSPIRATION

I am deeply grateful for the intellectual and inspirational light shared by the following researchers, authors, and visionaries. I encourage you to explore their work to deepen your own practice of *AWE - Awareness Wonder Expectancy: Now Consciously Create Your Personal Universe.*

This is a "Reader's Toolkit"

On Physics, the Quantum, and the Universe

Albert Einstein & Niels Bohr

Inspiration: For the foundational 20th-century debate on the nature of reality. Their clash over whether the universe is deterministic (*"God does not play dice"*) or probabilistic (The Copenhagen Interpretation) sits at the very heart of the Observe and Orient phases of the OOARR loop .

Stephen Hawking

Inspiration: For expanding our collective consciousness regarding the true scale of the macro-universe, the nature of time, and the event horizons that define our reality.

Sir Roger Penrose & Dr. Stuart Hameroff

For their ground-breaking work on the Orchestrated Objective Reduction (Orch OR) theory. Their collaboration—bridging the gap between a Nobel Laureate physicist and a clinical anesthesiologist—boldly proposes that consciousness is not merely a computation of the brain, but a fundamental quality of the universe itself, vibrating within the quantum microtubules of our cells. They remind us that the "music" of reality is played at a quantum level.

Dr. Mikko Partanen, Dr. Jukka Tulkki, and Professor Sorin Paraoanu

Inspiration: For their groundbreaking research (including work at Aalto University) into quantum thermodynamics, heat transport, and interaction-free measurements. Their exploration of how energy and information move through the quantum field provides modern scientific context for the concept of the Quantom and our Quan.

Charles Dickens

Books: A Tale of Two Cities ; A Christmas Carol

For his timeless mastery of observation and the "human algorithm." Long before neuroscience mapped the brain, Dickens mapped the human heart. His stories, particularly 'A Christmas Carol', serve as the ultimate case studies in neuroplasticity—showing us that no matter how entrenched our "Nervous Navigator" (Scrooge) may be, we all possess the capacity to wake up, re-write our story, and consciously create a new reality.

On the Neuroscience of the "Huddle"

Dr. Jill Bolte Taylor / Stephen Bartlett

Book: Whole Brain Living: The Anatomy of Choice and the Four Characters That Drive Our Life.

Watch/Listen: The Diary of a CEO with Steven Bartlett – Episode: "The Neuroscientist: The One Thing Everyone Should Know About The Brain." (This conversation was a profound confirmation of the AWE state).

Dr. Ethan Kross

Book: Chatter: The Voice in Our Head, Why It Matters, and How to Harness It. (Essential reading for managing the "Nervous Navigator").

Dr. Rick Hanson

Book: Hardwiring Happiness: The New Brain Science of Contentment, Calm, and Confidence. (The science behind the "20-second rule").

On Action, Mindset, "Atomic Habits" and "Let Them"

James Clear

Book: Atomic Habits and the creator of the popular "3-2-1" newsletter.

Mel Robbins

Book: The 5 Second Rule: Transform your Life, Work, and Confidence with Everyday Courage.

Concept/Guide: The "Let Them" Theory. (The foundational mindset for navigating the "20% field" of life).

Podcast: The Mel Robbins Podcast.

Mel deep dives into the "Let Them" theory and her interviews with Dr. Ethan Kross.

Jay Shetty

Book: Think Like a Monk: Train Your Mind for Peace and Purpose Every Day. (A key resource for the concepts of stillness and "10 minutes of boredom").

Podcast: On Purpose with Jay Shetty.

On Longevity, Wellbeing, Biology, and the "Sounding Board"

Dr. Peter Attia

Book: Outlive: The Science and Art of Longevity. (The definitive guide to the "Medicine 3.0" approach that informs the LiivWell protocols).

Podcast: The Peter Attia Drive.

Professor Andrew Huberman

Podcast: Huberman Lab. (The definitive resource for protocols on light viewing, sleep, and the "optical flow" mechanisms.

Watch: Andrew Huberman on YouTube.

Dr. William Li

Book: Eat to Beat Disease: The New Science of How Your Body Can Heal Itself.

Watch: Dr. William Li on YouTube (Angiogenesis and nutrition).

Professor David Sinclair

Book: Lifespan: Why We Age—and Why We Don't Have To.

Podcast: Lifespan with Dr. David Sinclair.

Dr. Halland Chen

Focus: Regenerative Medicine, High-Performance Health and Longevity.

Inspiration: Halland's insights on the 80/20 nature of wellbeing —the vital practice of maintaining high-performance health standards while allowing for the flexibility and flow of real life.

On AWE and the Universe

Charles Dickens

Book: A Tale of Two Cities

Dr. Dacher Keltner

Book: Awe: The New Science of Everyday Wonder and How It Can Transform Your Life.

Samantha Harvey

Book: Orbital. (Winner of the Booker Prize 2024. A beautiful meditation on the "Overview Effect").

EPILOGUE
FROM WAR TO PEACE—THE FRACTAL OF OUR FUTURE

As I write these closing words, I am struck by a realization that proves the very thesis of this book.

I did not plan for this journey to climax on Bondi Beach. When I began this manuscript on the rugged West Coast, staring out at the Indian Ocean, I had no outline that said, *"Finish at Bondi."* I did not script a geographical journey from West to East.

I simply set my intention. I oriented myself toward AWE Awareness Wonder Expectancy - and this is how the Universe responded. It co-created this ending with me, guiding the ripples of my life until Australia - and many in the world - found ourselves, figuratively or in person, standing, silent, hand-in-hand on the sands of Bondi Beach, looking out to the vast Pacific Ocean.

This unscripted transition—from the Indian to the Pacific—is a fractal of the quantum algorithm we use to create reality. It is a movement from the noise of the world to the signal of the soul.

Awareness: Beyond "Awake"

In the year 2025 - the year I wrote this book - we in our world found ourselves in a reality defined by its fractures and flaws. We witnessed the rise of what has aptly been called the "Word of the 2025": *Slop*

We saw it everywhere: The rhetorical slop of certain world leaders - even finding itself engraved in bronze by the then US President Trump disrespectfully below the pictures of past US Presidents; and the digital slop of social media.

We saw wars and rumours of wars.

I have more than hope - I have *Expectancy* - that, when you, my grandchildren, read this book, the world will have moved from "woke"— merely being awake to the surface-level symptoms of society - to being *Aware*.

Awareness is far deeper. It is understanding how our smallest choices, words and actions vibrate through the hidden, quantum levels of reality.

Every thought, every emotion, and every action we take is a pebble dropped into the universal ocean of possibilities - the Quantom.

These ripples travel and coalesce to form waves in *the universal ocean*, connecting us in ways we cannot see with the naked eye.

When we understand this connectivity, the illusion of separation vanishes. We realize that strangers are not "randoms" - they are simply people we haven't met yet.

There is no "other" to fight against. There are only potential connections waiting to be made.

When our ripples are born of anger or fear, they create dissonance.

When they are born of kindness and understanding, they harmonize to form a wave that we can surf together.

Wonder: The Co-Created Peace and Harmony

We have all and will all err in our lives, destabilizing our little boat - our wonderful *Quan*.

Engaging the wisdom available from the insights of Dr. Jill Bolte Taylor on the Whole Brain Huddle -imagined in this book as our personal crew - our Navigator, our Lookout/ Alarm, our Sensory Anchor, our Wise Visionary - will quickly right our boat - our *Quan*.

My own wrongs, in days long gone, led to estrangements from people I love - people I always will love. Estrangements I never wished for and never desired.

When we, as individuals, Orient and Re-Orient - with forgiveness, compassion, kindness and love - we move from strife and estrangement to reconciliation, we send Ripples through the Universe. These Ripples from just two are Fractals. The Ripples form waves. As individuals we are responsible for our Ripple in the Universe. We increase the possibilities to move to co-created peace around the world.

Expectancy: The Legacy of Love

This brings us to the final, vital element: *Expectancy*

Visualising Bondi Beach, at the edge of the Pacific, my Expectancy is not limited to my own life, nor is it limited to the turning of the calendar into 2026.

I am casting my intention far beyond the horizon. I hold a profound Expectancy for my children—Adam, Brett, and Jess— and for my beautiful grandchildren, Xanthe and Maddie, and any I am yet to know.

My hope is that they, all my family and future generations and all of you and those you Ripple with, will benefit from the wisdom I hope you discover in these pages.

We are the architects of that future. By refusing to engage in dissonance, only seeking harmony, kindness and love, we will co-create the beautiful, peaceful, abundant world we hope for.

Live in AWE

THE FRACTAL IN THE MOMENT

The path to personal joy and harmony with the universal is not a distant goal.

It is encoded and present in every moment of conscious choice.

Perhaps you are reading or listening to this as a skeptic.

You may believe, firmly, that materiality precedes consciousness. If so, that is a perfectly valid worldview.

The process of AWE Awareness Wonder Expectancy is still for you.

You do not need to believe in the metaphysics behind this process to benefit from awe.

Let's Reflect

Living in the "Observe - Act" trap is living a Newtonian life —a life of stimulus and response - just like a billiard ball, reacting to the last impact.

Living with AWE Awareness Wonder Expectancy and the OOARR Infinity Loop is choosing to live a Quantum life —a life of probabilities, expectancies and choices.

By pausing to Orient, you are engaging your higher-order consciousness to choose your response.

This practice is a more effective, resilient, and powerful operating system for a human mind, regardless of its origin. It works.

It is also important to be clear about what "works" means.

This is not an instant process.

This practice will not transform you overnight.

That is the "old world" Newtonian thinking.

This practice will do something deeper.

It will not turn you into someone else.

It will, finally, allow you to become you.

This is a path of adaptation, not perfection.

It is the 80/20 Rhythm.

You will "fail." You will fall back into the 20% reactive loop.

The goal is not to never fall.

The goal is to get better and better at "coming back" to your 80% rhythm.

We began this journey by showing how the universe can happen through you, not to you.

Every time you pause between observation and action to consciously Orient... Every time you fuel that pivot with Awareness, Wonder, and Expectancy...

Every time you choose to Reflect on your 20% rather than just react to it...and consider where your 80% can take you ... to one of many worlds - a new and better world - you are performing the same fundamental act of creation that the universe itself is striving to master.

The universe awakens one reflection at a time. And the next one is always yours.

AFTERWORD

Let's Co-Create Writing AWE was my way of observing and orienting to a new potential. Reading it was yours. If this book has resonated with you, if you have found a new sense of balance in your personal universe, your Quan, I invite you to share that reflection.Please consider taking a moment to leave a review online. Your "Active Reflection" not only helps me but signals to the algorithm that this message matters, helping it find the people who need it most.Let's co-create a better world, one review at a time.

A Bonus - Here's An Insight Into My Next Book

Thanks for posting your review- *Namaste*

In my next book I will be taking the Sullivan Theory, which has been about navigating life (the Quan), and extending it to the ultimate navigation: the transition out of biology.

The "Analog to Digital" metaphor you may recall from this book, AWE, is particularly striking—it bridges the tactile, friction-heavy nature of biological life with the pure, frictionless potential of the Quantom.

The Great Transduction

Thoughts for my next book: *"The Universal Interface"*

Throughout this book, we have explored how to use your input AWE (Awareness Wonder Expectancy) and your output OOARR (Observe Orient Act Realise Reflect) to navigate the Quantom in your wonderful "Quan" boat —to create your personal, experienced reality.

There remains the most profound question for each and every one of us, that every philosophy, science, and belief system must eventually face. The question of the end.

Or rather, the question of the shift.

As I refined The Sullivan Theory of the Universe, I had to confront the hardest part of the Quan: health challenges and physical pain. The inevitable breakdown of the biological machine. Even with Longevity Science making leaps and bounds, with suggestions of even hundreds of years of potential life. It is here, in the collision with mortality, that the theory finds its deepest grace.

Materiality is Not the Enemy

It is easy to resent the body when it hurts. It is easy to view gravity, the disease of aging, and limitation as prisons for our body, sometimes our mind and what about our consciousness, our spirit.

Consider this thought, which came to me in a moment of contemplation, I included in this book, when I was experiencing intense back pain:

"If you didn't 'feel' materiality, this would be death."

Exactly. In the Quantom (the infinite void of potential), there is no friction. There is no gravity. There is no pain. Because there is no friction, how could there be music.

Think of that violin string again. Without the tension (stress) and the violin bow creating friction (resistance), there is no sound. The string vibrates against the resistance to create the note. In this sense, materiality is not the enemy. It is the Sounding Board. Our bodies are the instruments that allow the infinite energy of the Quantom to be "played" as experience. We are here to feel the friction.

Death as an Orientation

So, what happens when the instrument breaks?

Current science offers us the Many Worlds Interpretation of quantum mechanics, suggesting that for every possible outcome, a universe exists.

I propose we look at this through the lens of OOARR (Observe Orient Act Realise Reflect).

Death is not a cessation. Death is simply a radical change in Orientation.

For your entire life, your consciousness has been Oriented toward the biological frequency. You have been transducing the energy of the universe through the dense filter of the five senses.

When the body ceases to function, I do not accept that we cease to be. We simply stop transducing through biology. We re-Orient from the Explicate Order (the physical world) back toward the Implicate Order (the Quantom).

From Analog to Digital

I am hoping the transition from life to afterlife will be like going from Analog to Digital.

Life is Analog. It is warm, rich, and tactile. Like a vinyl record though, it relies on friction. The needle must drag through the groove. It degrades over time. It has scratches, skips, and background noise (pain).

Consciousness is Digital. Consciousness is pure signal. No friction. No degradation. Perfect fidelity.

When we die, we are not erased. We are uploaded. We graduate from the friction of the groove to the purity of the signal. We move from being the instrument to being the music itself.

Play the Instrument While You Can

Can you "play" the universe without an instrument? Maybe. That is the mystery of the next phase.

For the time being, you have a body. You have the friction of the world. You have the ability to feel the sun, the wind, the ache of muscles, and the warmth of a hand.

Do not curse the friction. It is proof that you are currently in the Quan, actively transducing the miracle of existence.

So, until that final Orientation comes—until we make the leap from Analog to Digital—let us play this instrument with everything we have. Let us create a melody of AWE so profound that it echoes even after the instrument is put down.

In my next book, while I am going to explore the wisdom of the ancients, I am not going to ignore the physics, the cosmological and the biological.

ACKNOWLEDGEMENT

This book began, as all things do, with the Universe itself—the ultimate source of all potential.

Its boundless mystery is the wellspring of AWE (Awareness, Wonder, Expectancy), and it is in that spirit of gratitude I acknowledge the many people who have inspired, supported, and challenged me on this journey.

My deepest gratitude and love go to my family, my foundation.

To my wife, Marg. You are my co-creation partner.

This journey, and everything in it, is ours.

To my children, Adam, Brett, and Jess - my love for you is an unwavering source of inspiration and strength.

To my grandchildren, Xanthe and Maddie, and generations to come, you are a daily reminder of why this work matters—thank you for the inspiration, the awe, the wonder, and so much more. My profound thanks also to our grandchildren's wonderful mothers, Lou Monger and Alie Lambert, for their joyful, life affirming roles in our family's story.

To my brother, Steve, thank you for being so gentle, kind and courageous in the face of great challenges. To my other siblings, Terese, Ted, and Pete, I am grateful for your endurance as we navigated challenging times as children.

To all my aunts, uncles and cousins as well, you greatly influenced my life, almost but not quite to a person, in very positive ways - a few from my mum's side, alluded to in this book, in Gethsemanesque ways.

To my parents-in-law, Terry and Pat, thank you, above all, for Marg. Also for being examples to all, creating a generational legacy of harmony and cohesion. As one of your nine children said, "Everyone wants to be a Bolger". Thanks too for including the next generations of Sullivans in the tribe.

A life is measured by the community we keep, and I have been incredibly fortunate.

To all my friends, thank you for the conversations, the support, and the shared adventures.

In Australia:

LG "Brownie" Brown, Mark and Bernie Kelsey, Daniela Dlugocz, Carly Hinds, Aline Berder, Levi Clarke, El Bennett, Tricia Ray, Tony and Clare Ackland, Phil Baker, Brian Seth, Eric Konigsdorfer, David and Barbara Gray, Marty and Rose Kain, All the Seaslugs, All the Prev and Margs crew, the North Cottesloe Surf Club, Melville and Murdoch gym crews, the Riverview crew, the Chem Eng and Masters crews, my global kite surfing friends, Rob and Ania Cromb, Tim Healy, Mal Potts, Natalia Streltsova, Peter Lester, Greg and Cathy Meyerowitz, Meadowbank Youth Group friends and all the Class of 75/73.

Around the World:

France: David Lesage, Mimi Forestier, Yann Fontaine, Olivia Lai, Denise, Claude and Pascal Major , Alex Caizergues, Will Clarke, Elizabeth Rosinel, Noemie Ruelloux (Australia).

Bali / France: Pascale et Michel et Alissa et Chanael Doumeng.

Switzerland: Thierry et Marianne Moehr, Jitze et Stephanie Kramer, Katrin and Daniel

Köppell-Alge (and Katrin's parents, Franck and Cecile and boys,

Nico and Timo), Denton and Alexandra Knezovich, Jose Pont, Genevieve Chapuisat Pont, Markus and Sandra Widmer, Mirjam Martinez, Griso Martinez (Dominican Republic)

Switzerland / Australia: Richard and Mandy Swannell and all the Swannell tribe.

England: David Stanbridge, Suresh Rajan, Roger Frank.

Belgium: Guy Hellinx and Tim Engels (Italy).

Gibraltar: Gio Santini.

Singapore/ The Netherlands: Cris Heijckers, Maaike van Oostroom, Richard Barker.

Italy: Stefano Spreafico, Claudio Bonzanni

Denmark: Haldor Topsoe, Anja Nielsen, Bo Hartvigsen, Lene Hansen, Anne Mette Sorensen, Gabriel Antberg (Sweden), Rasmus Damsgaard.

USA: Roger Cusack, Paul Fabian, Steve Savage

Sweden: Tomas Johansson, Dag Rynell, Brian Goggin (Australia).

Estonia: Rein Saar (Australia).

Vanuatu: Joe Mala and all the Mala Family, Marty and Marg McAdam (Australia).

Dominican Republic: Laura De Leon

My Yoga teachers and friends:

Jo and Pepi Camponovo, Wendy Muir, Simon Borg Oliver.

My Tai Chi master

My friend, Rocky Kwong

To my startup adventurers and passionate friends -
who share vision and are open to taking risks:

USA: Ajay Yadav, Britt Chantel, and Rob Moore.

London: Professor Michael Mainelli, Cristiano Pizzocheri, Ava Kincsei, Dan Hinden, Kash Reid-Bashir, Laurent Sabatié, Raphael Caruso.

France: Mikael Quilfen, Romain Lavault

Australia: Michael Angie, Dimitri Bacopanos, Nat Carter, Adrian Boyce, Walt Sleator, Campbell Woskett.

Ireland: Dr. Terese O'Connor, Dee Lyons.

Vietnam: Professor Nguyen van Nguyen, Dr Tung Tran Dang, Dr. Tran Viet Hung (Australia).

Switzerland: Maya Bundt.

Romania: Roxana Vlad, Andre Olariu, Oana Vermesan

My contemplations on physics and cosmology
stand on the shoulders of giants:

Albert Einstein, Niels Bohr, Werner Heisenberg, Hugh Everett III, Von Neumann, Wigner, Stephen Hawking, Jukka Tulkki, Mikko Partanen, Karl Pribram, David Bohm.and Sir Roger Penrose.

Intellectual and Inspirational Light:

My thanks to Mel Robbins for her powerful insights on action and her and her daughter's "Let Them/Let Me" insights and author of the #1 New York Times bestselling book and Mel's wide ranging and wonderful YouTube podcasts.

Thanks to James Clear whose work, like mine, draws on biology, psychology, and neuroscience to create practical guides for behavior change. James' philosophy is grounded in the "Aggregation of Marginal Gains"—the mathematical certainty that small improvements (Micro) compound into remarkable results (Macro). He is the author of the #1 New York Times bestseller Atomic Habits and the creator of the popular "3-2-1" newsletter.

I am in awe of Dr. Jill Bolte Taylor, her recovery, her passion and for her profound explanations of the brain.

Thanks to Steven Bartlett for his globally successful, inspirational and deeply informative Diary of a CEO interviews with game changing thinkers from around the world.

Professor Andrew Huberman of Huberman Lab fame, and Professor David Sinclair for their wonderful, renowned approaches to sharing deep insights into being human and their vital research on human performance and longevity, and Dr. Peter Attia for his rigorous and very personally transparent approach to health and wellbeing.

My Philosophical and Educational Influences:

Providing Wisdom and inspiration along the way:

Father Massey (my Nana's brother), Father Bush, Father Alt, Father Murray, Father Rob Galea

Brother Raymond, Ray Maguire, Brother Darryl, Brother Elgar

Phil Baker, Phil Pringle, Phil Howell, Mal Potts, Tim Healy, Thierry et Marianne Moehr

From Sydney University: Professor Rolf Prince, Professor John Glastonbury, Dr. Barry Walsh.

From UWA: Professor Andre Maukel.

Bill Tai, Sir Richard Branson, Larry Lopez, Paula Taylor and my Necker Island Mai Tai catamaran co-crew.

Finally, I honour deeply those whose influence on my life is immeasurable and who have passed on:

John and Pauline Sullivan

Arthur and Marie McDermott

Mary and Ted Sullivan

ABOUT THE AUTHOR

John Sullivan

John Sullivan is a cosmologist, philosopher, and technologist whose life's work is dedicated to dissolving the artificial boundaries that have long separated science from spirit. He stands at a unique and necessary vantage point in the modern world: the convergence where the physics and measurable processes of our physical reality meet the boundless potential of human consciousness.

A graduate of both Sydney University and the University of Western Australia (UWA), John has spent decades charting a path that few dare to tread. His intellectual journey encompasses exploring the origins and processes of the universe and the fundamental laws of physics—and contemplating and applying these to navigate our daily lives.

Throughout his life, John became increasingly aware that we tend to view existence as something that happens to us, rather than a process we participate in.

To bridge this divide, John developed The Sullivan Theory of the Universe. This framework is not an abstract cosmological map nor some sort of self aggrandizement for John. The theory is a carefully considered synthesis of quantum mechanics, neuroscience, and biology, harmonized with the enduring wisdom of ancient spiritual traditions and non-dualistic philosophy.

The theory posits a radical yet empowering truth: we are not passive observers of a static reality. We are active co-creators of a dynamic energy field.

John's intention is to translate high-level metaphysical concepts —such as panentheism and the observer effect—into accessible, actionable "How-To" mechanics for daily living. He understands that for philosophy to be useful, it must be practical.

John's work seeks to empower everyone, including John, to stop reacting to the "Quantom" - the universal ocean of infinite possibilities - and start intentionally shaping it.

John's philosophy is deeply rooted in the physical landscape he calls home. Living in Prevelly, within the wild and pristine Margaret River region of Western Australia, he finds his daily rhythm in the raw, unpolished power of the Indian Ocean. For John, the ocean is more than scenery; it is a constant, living reminder of the state of AWE—the profound interconnectedness and majesty he invites his readers to inhabit. It is here, at the edge of the continent, that he finds the stillness necessary to decode the noise of the modern world.

When he is not writing, contemplating the physics of existence, John is grounded by the simple, profound beauty of his own personal reality. He can be found walking the coast with his lovely bride, Marg or sharing the wonder of the natural world with his children and grandchildren - and his friends and family.

In a world often divided by dogma and data, John Sullivan offers a third way: a unified vision seeking to amplify the values of love, kindness, grace, and compassion in our world.- where every individual consciousness is awakened to their power to co-create a life of AWE Awareness Wonder Expectancy.

www.ingramcontent.com/pod-product-compliance
Lightning Source LLC
Chambersburg PA
CBHW022005090426
42741CB00007B/898